EXTENDED FAMILIES
a memoir of India

EXTENDED FAMILIES

a memoir of India

VEN BEGAMUDRÉ

COTEAU BOOKS

Edited by Dave Margoshes
Book designed by Tania Craan
Cover portrait hand coloured by the author
Typeset by Susan Buck
Printed and bound in Canada

Library and Archives Canada Cataloguing in Publication

Begamudré, Ven, 1956-, author
    Extended families : a memoir of India / Ven Begamudré.

Issued in print and electronic formats.
ISBN 978-1-55050-927-4 (softcover).--ISBN 978-1-55050-928-1 (PDF).
--ISBN 978-1-55050-929-8 (EPUB).--ISBN 978-1-55050-930-4 (Kindle)

    1. Begamudré, Ven, 1956- --Family. 2. Begamudré, Ven, 1956-
--Childhood and youth. 3. East Indian Canadians--Biography. 4.
East Indians--Canada--Biography. 5. Authors, Canadian (English)--
Biography. 6. India--Biography. 7. Canada--Biography. I. Title.

PS8553.E342Z46 2017   C813'.54   C2017-903992-X
                                     C2017-903993-8

2517 Victoria Avenue
Regina, Saskatchewan
Canada S4P 0T2
www.coteaubooks.com

Available in Canada from:
Publishers Group Canada
2440 Viking Way
Richmond, British Columbia
Canada V6V 1N2

10 9 8 7 6 5 4 3 2 1

Coteau Books gratefully acknowledges the financial support of its publishing program by: the Saskatchewan Arts Board, The Canada Council for the Arts, the Government of Saskatchewan through Creative Saskatchewan, the City of Regina. We further acknowledge the [financial] support of the Government of Canada. Nous reconnaissons l'appui [financier] du gouvernement du Canada.

I think I write because I have something to say that I fail to say satisfactorily in conversation, in person. Then there are things like conceit, stubbornness, a desire to retaliate on those who have hurt me paralleled by a desire to repay those who have helped me, a need to try to create something which may live after me (which I take to be the detritus of the religious feeling), the sheer technical joy of forcing almost intractable words into patterns of meaning and form that are uniquely (for the moment at least) mine, a need to make people laugh with me in case they laugh at me, a desire to codify experience, to come to terms with things that have happened to me, and to try to tell the truth (to discover what is the truth) about them. And I write especially to exorcise, to remove from myself, from my mind, the burden of having to bear some pain, the hurt of some experience: in order that it may be over there, in a book, and not in here in my mind.

— B.S. Johnson, Introduction to
Aren't You Rather Young To Be Writing Your Memoirs?

For my extended family

⇛ TABLE OF CONTENTS ⇚

PART 3

Amma, My Mother

BONUS MATERIALS

Author's Note

You may read this book in any order you choose. However, it would be best if you read the three chapters about my mother in order. The present of this book is 1991, which was the year I turned thirty-five, while the past of this book is 1977, which was the year I turned twenty-one.

This memoir of my family, and my pursuit of my own identity within the family, is based on the journal I kept during my first visit to India, in 1977–78 – my first visit back to the country of my birth that I left when I was six. Among other notable events during that visit was a stay of several months with my father, who had moved back to India after some twenty years in Canada. It was the first time that I had lived with him as an adult. And, as it turned out, it would also be the last time I saw my mother, who had also returned to India.

– Ven Begamudré, April 2017

The Year I Turned Twenty-One

FATHER: What are you planning to do when you graduate?
ME: I'd like to become a writer.
FATHER: If you're serious about it, go ahead.
MOTHER: You said you wanted to be a civil servant; your
    father helped you get through college; and now you
    want to write? What do you have to write about?
FATHER: Tolstoy wrote about his family.

At Thirty-Five

A POET: What exactly is this new book about?
ME: At first I wanted revenge. I don't care anymore.
    Now it's because I need to forgive them. Or maybe
    I just want to see how many different ways I can write
    the truth.
A POET: Write that down. Remember it.

PART ONE

How My Great-Grandfather Lost His Land,
and Other Familiar Twists of Fate

My father's sisters, Mani (standing at left) and Ratna (seated at right), with my grandmother, Bhagirathi (seated at left), in the 1930s; separating Bhagirathi and Ratna is Ratna's father-in-law, R. Seshagiri-Rao. Ohters unidentified.

ROYAL ORCHID SERVICE

Friday, September 30, 1977

I REACH HEATHROW at 7:10 a.m. by airport bus. I'm late but my flight's been delayed an hour and a quarter. Devon breakfast: scones under clotted cream topped with strawberry jam. Nothing interesting to get Grandma as a present. "Thai International's Royal Orchid Service" they call this flight, bound for Bangkok via Karachi. This is the cheapest flight I could get. Hostesses give us purple orchids. Then our plane sits on the runway till 12:30 p.m., thanks to a slowdown by air traffic controllers.

The last time I left London by plane I was with my mother. It was August of 1962, when I was six. We had stopped here for three days on our way from India to Canada. This is what I remember of London: pudding and pie. I kept asking for them because of the song:

Georgie Porgie, pudding and pie,
Kissed the girls and made them cry.

As far as I knew, Georgie Porgie came from England; so did Polly, who put the kettle on; so did the Three Blind Mice and every other character in the English nursery rhymes we'd sung in my Indian school. I didn't want to kiss any girls and make them cry but, if we were going to stop in England, I wanted pudding and pie. I got my pudding in a little restaurant with tables full of men. It was likely English pudding, thick and full of raisins and nuts, but I would always remember it as my first taste of the smooth chocolatey puddings of Canada. These came from boxes marked Jello and Shirriff. As for the pie, I didn't get that during our stay in London; I got it on the BOAC flight to Canada. The flight stopped at Shannon, Ireland, and perhaps even Gander, Newfoundland. This wasn't real pie, not like the huge pies of Canada that had to be sliced into triangular wedges and sometimes topped with ice cream. This was a lemon tart served as part of the meal I ate from my airplane tray. But my mother said, "There, you have your pie at last," and I believed her. She had a gift for keeping little boys happy.

This is also what I remember of London: we went on a guided bus tour and I fell asleep. The driver kept an eye on me while the guide led more energetic tourists about the sites. I remember waking once and watching, through the window, while my mother came down broad steps from what might have been the British Museum.

Finally, I remember the bed and breakfast in which we stayed on the second floor. There was carpeting in the hallway, something I had rarely seen in India. The wood was dark and the walls were covered with pictures. Milk came in bottles on the doorstep instead of being poured by the milkman into a vessel held by the servant. There were no servants here but there was a telephone, in the downstairs hallway. One evening, as we got ready for bed, we heard the telephone ring. The kind woman who owned the house fetched my mother and I sat on the carpeted steps to watch her speak on the phone. She looked pleased. It was one of her uncles, a brother of her father. I don't remember meeting this London uncle. She looked so pleased, I thought that the man on the phone was my father, calling from Canada to make sure everything was all right.

I would soon meet my father again. I had met him for the first time when I was four and he'd visited us in India. Now I barely remembered him. I did remember writing him an aerogramme just before we left India and asking if he would be meeting us in a Chevrolet. That's what rich people in India seemed to drive: Chevrolets. In fact, it turned out that he drove a Ford. A green and white '58 Ford Fairlane. It was splendid. On the day we met in Canada, at Dorval Airport in Montreal, I wore a belted, brown suit my mother had bought me in London. The suit came with a matching cap. I must have looked like a little English gentleman, not at all what my father must have been expecting. I don't remember wearing that suit and cap after landing in Canada.

All of that was fifteen years before this, my first India trip, in August of 1962. The last time I left London. With my mother.

I'M IN THE WINDOW SEAT on the left side. The couple next to me are fun. He's a New Zealander with a stud in his left ear and turquoise bracelets on his wrists. He owns a souvenir boutique on Carnaby Street. She's English. They're already drinking. He's flipping through a *Playboy*; she's flipping through a *Playgirl*. She oohs over the *Playgirl* centrefold and he asks, "Want to see mine?" She elbows him and says, "I'd rather see it in action." They include me in their twosome by offering me a drink. I sound stuffy when I refuse. Good thing it doesn't put them off. I'm getting tired of travelling alone (by bus and train) for five weeks: London, Salisbury, Caernarvon, London, Inverness, Oban, York, London.

I came back to London from Caernarvon to change my plans. I'd booked myself on a Transit bus tour – the India overland trip by bus – against my dermatologist's wishes. He'd said my chronically dry skin might not stand up to so much travelling, and he'd been right. Even with all the cortisone cream I had – two or three different kinds – I kept scratching my skin. And so, two weeks into my five-week tour of Britain, I'd returned to London to cancel my booking to India overland. Transit had refunded two-thirds of my payment, enough for a cheap plane ticket. I've had so many dermatologists – and will have for another five years – that I won't remember this one's name for long. I will remember it had an *itch* sound in it: Mitchell or Richards. And I would always remember the quilted wall-hanging in his waiting room. Someone must have made it especially, that bright, handmade quilt with its decidedly unpoetic warning:

IF YOU PICK IT
IT WON'T HEAL!

FIRST STOP – AMSTERDAM, thirty-five minutes after takeoff. Canals and waterways throughout the city and countryside; red-roofed houses and one grotesquely immense apartment building. A passable lunch, better than the one on British Airways coming over from Toronto. The Thai hostesses wear red or purple outfits with shiny stoles. All announcements are in Thai – sounds like Chinese but uses a lot of r's – and English, stilted. Fly over mountains that might be the Pyrenees. Sun casts shadows that turn the land into a relief map in greens and browns. I try to relax. Take off my self-winding Seiko and put it in the pocket of my new plum-brown suit jacket,

My paternal grandfather, Krishna (front row, third from left), about 1932 when he was executive engineer in Hasan district for the Public Works Department of Mysore State.

bought on Oxford Street. I fold the jacket and put it under my seat. This feels better. Accept a drink towards evening and even a cigarette. I don't fall asleep, though; play solitaire with borrowed cards. We fly over Tehran: large, crescent-shaped harbourfront with a high peak in the background. I'm sure I can make out the odd mosque, minarets floodlit. If I'd taken the Transit tour, I would have been able to see Tehran from the ground. On my way to India – overland.

LOCKSEAL

My paternal grandfather, Krishna, superintending engineer with the Mysore Public Works Department, about 1940.

IN KANNADA, the language outsiders call Kanarese, *beega* means lock. *Mudre*, pronounced *moodh-ray*, means seal.

A long time ago, no one knows quite how long, a man who worked as the guardian of the treasury in the palace of the Wodeyars, the South Indian maharajas of Mysore, took the name Beegamudre, literally Lockseal. Each night when he closed the treasury, he followed a painstaking ritual. He secured the bolt on the treasury door with a padlock. Around this he sewed a scrap of white silk into a bag. Then he dripped red wax along the seams. Onto each circle of wax, he stamped the royal seal of the Wodeyars, which was then, itself, locked away. During his tenure, the treasury was never broken into; but, true, the ritual would not actually have prevented determined thieves from a robbery. They could have bribed the guards, after all, or overpowered them, and picked or broken the lock. But no matter how carefully the thieves might have re-sewn the silk over the lock, they could not have duplicated the royal seal. In the morning, when the guardian arrived to unlock the treasury, he would know it had been robbed for he would find the seals broken. Lock, seal: *beegamudre*.

When the man grew too old, when his eyes grew too weak and his fingers too shaky to thread his needle and sew the scrap of silk, he stopped going to the palace. His son, who inherited his job, saw little glamour in locking and unlocking a door, even if it did lead to a treasury, and he began to dream of finding a treasure of his own.

One day, some distance northeast of Mysore City, someone discovered gold. It was in a district called Kolar, in what came to be known as the Kolar Gold Fields, and so this younger Beegamudre moved his wife and children and his aged parents to Kolar District; to a village called Nelawanki. As was the custom in parts of rural India, the family adopted the name of its village and came to be called the Nelawanki Beegamudres. The old man who had once locked the treasury door and sealed the scrap of silk died dreaming of the day he would arrive to find the seals broken. Perhaps, though, he died of disappointment, for his son found no gold in Nelawanki. The nearest gold was in the next village, or the next, and so the younger Beegamudre, who could not face returning to Mysore City, became a farmer. The ground was arid and the soil was thin. It yielded nothing more valuable than groundnuts. But over time, perhaps even generations, the groundnuts themselves brought a fortune – if not in gold, at least in silver. The family found itself owning much of the land surrounding the village. Where once the family had become the Beegamudres of Nelawanki, now the village became the Nelawanki of the Beegamudres.

By the late nineteenth century, the head of the family and of the village was a man called Subbha-Rao. One of his tasks was to collect taxes, which he handed over to the seniormost official in the district, an *Angrez* (an Englishman) called by his title: the Collector. In return for this task, Subbha-Rao received a horse and an annual stipend of sixty rupees. Owning so much land and dealing with the Collector made Subbha-Rao proud, perhaps even vain. When the time came for his two eldest sons to begin secondary school, he sent them all the way to Madras, on the east coast. Their names were Seshagiri-Rao, or Sesha, and Ramachandra-Rao, or Rama.

In Madras they fell under the spell of a *maistry* (an overseer). Burma was at this time a province of India. Wages were higher in Burma, where the economy was booming, than in South India, so it was easy for *maistries* to recruit young men to work in and around Rangoon. Even after selling their schoolbooks, Sesha and Rama could not afford their passage. No matter, the *maistry* told them. He would lend them the fare and they could repay him over time. True, Sesha and Rama did earn high wages, labouring in construction and so on; but, no matter how much they earned, they found themselves unable to discharge their debt. The *maistry* charged them interest on the fare and also deducted the cost of room and board from their wages. Room was space enough for a bedroll in a large hut that was noisy with men. Board was three meals a day, which the men themselves cooked. Sesha and Rama found themselves in Rangoon not as free men but as indentured labourers. They earned a good living, if only on paper, and they promised Subbha-Rao they would send money home. He was furious, but he could do little to them.

He could, however, take his fury out on his one daughter and on the youngest of his four children, also a boy. Subbha-Rao warned the boy never to be dishonest. Ever.

It soon became clear that the longer Sesha and Rama worked, the farther they would sink into debt. Subbha-Rao could not bear this. He had to think of his good name. Swearing that no son of his would remain indentured for life, Subbha-Rao sold his land. All of it. Though he paid off their debts, he never saw either Sesha or Rama again, for he died shortly after this – of shame.

His widow, Ammiah, pondered her family's fate. If she remained in Nelawanki, her youngest son would have to leave school and find work and would never earn his SSLC, his Secondary School Leaving Certificate, and if her late husband had been proud of his good name, he had been even more proud of his ability to read and write English. He had had to do this in order to represent the village to the Collector and the Collector to the village. Ammiah decided to move with her daughter and one remaining son west to Bangalore. It was the largest city in Mysore State. Shortly after her move, she married her daughter off to a pleader (a lawyer). The main thing now was to ensure that Ammiah's only son, for this was how she sometimes thought of him, finished school.

His name was Krishna-Rao. His full name should have been Nelawanki Beegamudre Krishna-Rao, but he did not belong to Nelawanki any more than it belonged to him. He dropped the name of the village and, for some reason, also dropped one of the three e's in Beegamudre. Krishna, the boy born in Nelawanki, the boy whose brothers had run away to Burma – this Krishna became the first Begamudré. Many years later, when he was nearly sixty-five, he became my grandfather.

—⋇—

MY FATHER, KRISHNA'S SON, would have told parts of this story differently. He did, in fact, tell parts of it differently. I have never questioned him about it, and I do not intend to question him now. The times I would have listened patiently to his stories, the times I might have questioned him directly – such times have passed. It may simply be that he filled gaps for himself the way I have filled other gaps for myself while reconstructing Subbha-Rao's standing in Nelawanki according to what one of my cousins told me. This was during my second visit to India, in 1988. I have wanted to tell his story ever since my first visit, eleven years before – a visit during which I nearly died and my mother did die.

In my father's version, Subbha-Rao did not own all the land in Nelawanki. He owned a mere fifteen acres. He held the title of village headman because he knew how to read and write English. And I must confess that I have reconstructed what happened to his eldest sons through my less-than-thorough reading of Burmese history. Here is my father's version of how Subbha-Rao lost his title and his land:

Burma was at this time a province of India and Sesha and Rama heard about wondrous opportunities awaiting them in Rangoon. The boys thus sold their schoolbooks to buy their passage. In Rangoon they found plenty of work because Burmese men were more interested in gambling than in working. However, Sesha and Rama also began gambling. They fell so deeply into debt that they faced being thrown into prison. Their father swore that no son of his would ever go to prison, and so he sold his land and his title as village headman. He never saw either Sesha or Rama again, for he died shortly afterwards, of a broken heart.

I have only my father's word for what happened to Sesha and Rama after Subbha-Rao disposed of his land. It may be that I will discover, from yet another cousin, that parts of what followed should be told differently. But it rings true enough to me. During that first trip back, I asked some of my relatives how to contact the "Burmese" branches of our family. Everyone claimed that they did not know. One or two were less protective. "You don't want anything to do with them," I heard. "They are all mad."

About the time that my grandfather Krishna married, his eldest brother Sesha died, young, in Rangoon – but not before entrusting his son to my grandfather's care. Even as Krishna began his own family, he found himself also raising a nephew as his own son. There may even have been a girl; if so, I know nothing of her. The boy, Nagesha, is now the oldest surviving Begamudré. He is a tall man, taller than others of his generation. During my first visit back, I met him and his wife in Mysore City. They lived in a house called, appropriately enough, Beegamudre House. With three e's.

The second of Subbha-Rao's sons, Rama, stayed in Rangoon for the time being. His wife bore him five children. Five who lived, that is. Each time she became pregnant, she returned to Madras to deliver her child. She took deck passage and many a woman gave birth in mid-journey. Sometimes, if the child was born dead, the midwife dropped the body over the side while the mother screamed. Child after child bobbed in the wake. This was how Rama's wife went mad, or so my father claims. He remembers her as sharp-tongued and hysterical. But even if she did not go mad, one of her children found himself in the midst of madness.

During the depression, Burmese Chettyars, Indian bankers from Madras, foreclosed on millions of acres of Burmese land. The aspirations of Burmese nationalists soon focused on the actions of all Indians in Burma, whether labourers or financiers. Even after Burma separated from India in the mid-1930s, millions of Indians lived in the former province. One of them

was Rama's eldest son. I shall call him BB, for Burmese Beegamudre, though BB sounds uncomfortably close to VB, which
is what my father calls me. BB had his own family by now, and
although his brothers and sisters had returned to India with
their parents – Rama and his troubled wife – BB had not.

Even as Japan prepared to invade Burma in the dying
weeks of 1941, many Burmese nationalists saw the impend-
ing invasion as a way of freeing their country from both the
British sahib and the Indian banker. When the Japanese invaded Lower Burma in early 1942, they expelled all the Indians. BB had already sent his wife and children back to
Madras, but he was unable to reach India by sea. He found
himself among the half million Indians who were trying to
reach home on foot. This meant a trek of some six hundred
and fifty kilometres from Rangoon to the gateway to Upper
Burma, a city called Mandalay. Sometimes his route followed
the Irrawaddy River, which waters the paddies of Lower
Burma; sometimes his route left the river for dense forest.
When Japanese planes strafed the trunk road or highway,
refugee columns turned into screaming, fleeing mobs.

At first, British soldiers helped the refugees; but with the
monsoons of late spring approaching, the soldiers abandoned
their charges. The soldiers made for the Chindit Hills on the
India-Burma border. Both of my Burmese guidebooks refer to
the British retreat without mentioning the Indian refugees.
Military historians have written about this retreat in more
detail. The soldiers, many with their feet wrapped in rags,
plodded across the border. They knew that if they did not
reach India before the monsoon arrived, they would be cut
off when the border valleys filled with rain – rain so heavy
that it turned into flowing water so swift it could uproot trees.
According to one account, a British general waited on a hill
in India while his men limped past him to safety. On the day

the monsoon began, he turned his back on Burma; he even turned his back on his men. Meanwhile, no longer escorted by soldiers, BB and other Indians also made for the border. Half a million Indians had set out from Lower Burma; half of them died along the way. BB would have been in his early twenties but the trek turned his hair white. So my father says. BB rejoined his wife and children in Madras, and they left South India, likely for the North. No one knows where. I should say, instead, that no one will say. For good reason, since four of Rama's children – BB's brothers and sisters – died tragically, by their own hands. One, a classmate of my father, was prone to epilepsy. During one of his seizures, my father says, his cousin took sleeping pills. An elder brother drowned himself in a reservoir called Malleswaram Tank. Both of the sisters had unhappy marriages. One sister hanged herself in her bathing room. The other moved to Bombay with her husband and threw herself into the sea. Like all of her stillborn siblings, she sank and then rose to bob in the waves. I am not sure what happened to BB; I would like to think that he died of old age and rejoined the friends he had left on the road to Mandalay.

"You don't want anything to do with them," I heard. "They are all mad."

There we have it: how my great-grandfather lost his land and other familiar twists of fate.

And here is the prologue of an epic novel that I began during my first trip back. I never finished the novel although I did write one of the later chapters, set in 1947 during the partition of India and Pakistan. The very concept of an epic reminds me of the stories my father liked to tell; the style reminds me too much of his style.

The prologue is handwritten on pages pulled from a notebook, six inches by eight, bound in blue. Among other things, the cover bears this:

WISDOM
Manufactured out of
WHITE PRINTING PAPER
Exercise Book
Retail Price not to exceed Rs. 1.05 (Inclusive Cover)
Local taxes extra

The price has been overstamped Rs. 1.18 in purple ink. Below Wisdom is a generic school crest. It contains a wind instrument and a music book, a flask and two test tubes, an artist's palette and brush, a micrometer measuring a gear. The white paper was off-white even when the book was new.

"Nomads: Prologue" (Autumn 1977)

While most men are content to live and die in their native land, some leave to find greater happiness. Often their journeys are short. But those who leave to escape unhappiness travel far because, like nomads in a desert, they leave every oasis lured by the promise of a distant mirage.

These thoughts occupied the mind of Nelawanki Gopal Raja while he awaited the birth of his fourth child. If the child lived, Raja would father no more. Four children were enough for a man with only ten acres of land. He wondered whether this last child would be a boy or a girl. If a boy, there would be that much less land to divide between his sons. If a girl, he would face the problem of finding a suitable husband for her.

Three years earlier, Raja had given his first and only daughter to the son of a neighbour. The girl had been ten, the boy eleven. Shortly before the wedding, Raja's wife had given birth to their third child, a boy. The birth of a son and the marriage of a daughter had made that year, 1919, a memorable year, if not always a happy one. Alas, the young bridegroom died soon after the wedding, leaving the bride a widow and she never had a chance to live with her husband.

Two other events had made 1919 a highly memorable year. One had been the signing of a peace treaty somewhere in France. It had signalled the end of "the war to end all wars." Raja liked that phrase. The other had been a massacre in a northern city called Amritsar. It had signalled the beginning of the end of British rule in India. Still, nothing had changed: wars continued breaking out; the Raj survived.

Raja secretly pitied his fellow villagers. Births, deaths and marriages were the only notable events in their lives of routine hardship. However, life was more exciting for him because he understood world affairs. Although he considered himself an educated man, he was only literate. His knowledge of the world beyond his valley came from week-old issues of *The Hindu*. He had not even been to ~~Bangalore~~ Madras, the city where it was printed. Since he was the only man in the village with an ability, however limited, to read and write English, Raja was its *karnam*. Once a year, he collected taxes and held them for the *thaluk*.

Raja disliked the task. In a poor place like Nelawanki, tax collection was a frustrating business. Few people earned enough through selling the produce of their farms to pay any tax. Raja knew that the District Collector suspected him of withholding a portion of the moneys, but Raja was one of the few *karnams* who did not. He was content with his annual stipend and the gift of a horse. The sixty rupees was enough to feed his family, but the horse was now of little use. Once, he had ridden it through the village and surrounding countryside on the days he collected taxes. Now the horse was lame and blind. Raja ~~pulled it behind him~~ led it by a rope. The animal was a symbol of his rank: like the rolled-up, out-of-date newspaper he carried

17

under his arm when he visited anyone. Reflecting on the poverty in the village brought his thoughts back to emigration. His family was the only one in Nelawanki that knew its lineage. Gopal was no unusual name in a country where herding cows was a common vocation. Gopals are the Smiths of South India, and Raja's household claimed descent from court herders. Moreover, they had a famous ancestor in the person of Raghavendra Swami, one of the great ~~faith healers~~ mystics of India. And the Gopal lineage extended well beyond the fifteenth century yogi. In the eighth century after the birth of Christ, a dozen families had migrated from Persia, through Afghanistan and into India. One of them was the Beegamudre tribe.

Raja's maternal grandfather had been a Beegamudre, a guardian of the king's treasury. Every evening he had closed the doors, wrapped a cloth around the lock, and sealed it with wax. The first Beegamudres had been of Aryan stock, taller and fairer than the Dravidians of South India. Even centuries of intermarriage had not completely dissipated the strain. Raja examined his hands. In truth, was he not fairer than most other villagers? Some of them were almost as dark as untouchables.

He could not understand why his ancestors had eventually settled in this particular valley. Perhaps they had hoped to find gold here. But when they had found that the gold fields of Kolar did not extend this far, why had they not moved on? Farming was a poor substitute for mining when there was little water and only groundnuts could grow. Had his ancestors come here in search of happiness? If so, they had found it, in some form, here in Nelawanki. Or had they come here to escape unhappiness? If so, their settlement here was but a brief respite. One day, the Gopals would move on, but Raja would never do so willingly. He would be content to die ~~in Kolar District~~ here.

A voice asked, "Appa, what are you doing?"

Raja opened his eyes. His daughter, Usha, stood before

him. On either side of her was one of his sons. The elder, Srinivas, held her hand while he stared at Raja. Younger, naked Krishna was perched on Usha's hip. He saw only the banana poking from Raja's pocket.

"I was thinking," Raja replied. He peeled the fruit and divided it into four pieces, three of them for his children.

"So, you are eating again!" a shrill voice exclaimed.

Raja turned to confront his wife's mother. "There is no shortage of food in our house," he said. "Thank God." He threw the peel to one of his cows. The other cows slept.

"If you call this hut a house!" she exclaimed. "You may go inside now. Rani has given you another son." The woman scowled at Usha.

The girl lowered her gaze and wandered away with Krishna on her hip.

"Do you still wish to find her another husband? Who will marry a widow?"

Raja shrugged. "There is no hurry," he said. "It was ill luck that the boy died before she could join him. It was not her fault."

"Still, she should live with her father-in-law's people, not with ours."

Raja clucked his tongue. "*Thi!* The boys would cry if I sent her away."

The woman spat red juice at Raja's feet. "*Thup!* Do you want to see your newest son or will you stay here and think some more?"

"I will come." Raja took a last look at the cloudless sky. Preparations would have to be made for the naming ceremony. For a third time, he would write a boy's name in sacred rice. This time, it would be Rama, after the god-king of Ayodhya.

"Where is my son?" Raja called, entering his house. "Where is my prince?"

Missing Arnold Brown

Saturday, October 1, 1977

WE REACH KARACHI 10:00 p.m. London time; it's 4:00 a.m. here. This airport is not what I'd expected, and part of it's still under construction. The Third World is always under construction. No wonder the clerk at PIA (Pakistan International Airways) in London smiled when I said I would wait in the airport all night for my connecting flight. The place is bare, and hot even with the few ceiling fans. Two types of people: ordinary folk in different outfits, men in uniform. Different uniforms too. Officials in white with blue and gold rank badges on epaulettes. Policemen in blue with silver pips on their epaulettes. Soldiers, mostly privates, carry old rifles and guard entrances to various sections. I don't mind the rifles. Know how to use one, though the ones I can fire and strip are semi-automatic FN CI's from my army reserve days in Canada. It's the soldiers who make me nervous. They carry their Lee-Enfields as if they don't know which end is which.

False start after false start. Sent by the Special Handling Office to the SAS representative of Thai International. Can't issue me a hotel voucher because I'm travelling on a discontinued ticket. Ten-minutes' walk from the airport is a motel-like affair called The Inn. A bearer wheels my suitcase down a verandah and rouses a sleeping man. It's so muggy that I'm sweating in my fine, wool jacket. Room's clean, although not sumptuous. Better than the Transit Hotel in London; more expensive too: 190 rupees (now about twenty-five dollars). "I am room boy," the man says. Salutes at the door. Won't take an English coin because he can't change it. "You have cigarette?" he asks.

Shrugging off my apologies, he makes an about-face. Tell him I'll leave his tip with the daytime room boy after I change my money in the morning. Tell him: make sure to wake me at 11:30 a.m.; my Bombay flight is 5:15 this afternoon.

I lock the door and place an armchair against it. Wash and go to bed. Try to ignore the odd mosquito, its buzzing drowned by a noisy air conditioner. Realize finally I'm in Asia. Am retracing the general route Mom and I took in August 1962. Only then it was Bangalore-Bombay-Karachi-London-Montreal. We stayed a few nights in Bombay and London but not in Karachi. No one knows I've stopped here overnight. Indians still claim that Pakistanis like to throw Indians in jail. My Air Canada flight bag is coming in handy.

BROAD DAYLIGHT when I awake. My watch says 4:45. I remember shouting in my sleep at someone at the door. Must have been the daytime room boys trying to wake me at 11:30 like I said. Shit, shit, shit. Lunge into action. Throw on my clothes and repack in five minutes. (Forget my dressing gown in the closet. Some tip: a blue acetate with red and gold paisley; a lot cheaper than it looks, but they won't know that.) Shout, "Boy, boy!" Order one to run behind with my suitcase, another to get a taxi. Pay my bill in pounds. The brown plastic clock on the reception desk reads 8:05. Must be broken, like so much else in the Third World. Run to the taxi. We're at the airport in two minutes. Crowds everywhere, half inside the terminal, half pressed against the glass front. A soldier holding his rifle across his chest blocks the door. "Out of my way!"

I grab the rifle with both hands and shove him aside. Run to a counter, with the soldier on my heels. Flash my ticket in an official's face. "I'm on the flight to Bombay," I say. Not calmly.

The soldier stands there not knowing what to do. Finally drifts away.

The official examines my ticket. Slowly. "But, sir," he says, "the flight is at 5:15 p.m."

"I know that!"

"It is now only nine o'clock in the morning."

That clock wasn't broken. My watch had stopped. The self-winding Seiko I'd put in my jacket pocket under my Royal Orchid seat. He expects me to feel embarrassed but I laugh and so does he. Now what?

Eat. A scanty meal in the Sky-something restaurant on the second floor. No people in native outfits here. Only officials in white uniforms and civilians in suits. Strong coffee served in a silvery pot with a dented lid. Thick toast that's tough to chew. Glass of cold water. Can't stay here all day. I need a plan. Simple: take a taxi into the city to a good European hotel and wait there in comfort.

Downstairs, a driver leads me across the street to his parked cab. Wait for him to back out. A bearded man appears. Behind him: an old woman, her head covered with the end of her brown sari. "Please, sir," he says. "This is my mother."

"No," I tell him.

"But sir, this is my mother. I am in trouble."

Aren't we all.

Driver's son comes with us in the cab. The fare is fifty rupees (about six dollars). This supposedly cheap route to Bangalore might cost just as much as flying directly. Or maybe not. The long road to town is Shah-something Road. They drive on the left here. Driver ignores the lanes, honks others out of his way. Scooters; trucks with gaily painted backboards; autorickshaws with fancy canopies: pink, yellow, blue. Road's lined with houses. "Townhouses," the driver calls them. Look like they're rotting even where they stand. Palm trees, other vegetation, more rotting townhouses. A billboard advertises the only five-star hotel in Karachi.

"Take me to the Intercontinental," I say.

What an oasis. The doorman wears a tunic and turban; so do the bellboys, who look like page boys. All the eyes are drawing me to the reception desk. Think fast. I tell the clerk: "I'm here to meet Mr. Arnold Brown."

Why Arnold Brown, of all things? Because he's head of the Salvation Army in Canada. Just what I need right now.

The clerk checks his register. "We have a Mister A. Brown," he says.

"He always uses Arnold," I say. "From Canada."

"I am sorry, we have no reservation for a Mr. Arnold Brown."

"It must be under his wife's name."

"And what is his wife's name?"

"I don't know. They just got married. She's Pakistani. Tell you what. You look after my luggage and I'll just wait for him. You don't mind?"

"Not at all, sir."

I need a wash. Change my underwear and socks in a toilet cubicle. Always carry spares in my flight bag. Now I have to change more money but the hotel cashier refuses because I'm not a guest. Sure I am. And the bank nearby is closed. I stand at the entrance, keep trying to get in. A fat cab driver offers to change money for me. Have to say no half a dozen times, then have to be sharp. Another bank across the intersection. Same story. Doors are open but the bank closed ten minutes ago. "How far is American Express?" Half a mile. I try another bank. "How far is American Express?" Three miles. Sweating, I return to the hotel. A bellboy takes me back to the first bank and an official changes ten pounds. It'll have to do.

Back to the hotel for a shave. First time I've let a barber shave me. Straight razor too. I live. In the lounge, try reading Hemingway's *Islands in the Stream* but give up. At noon, a sandwich and orange juice, freshly squeezed. Outside the coffee shop is a pool. People – westerners – swim and lounge. Start reading Orwell's *Burmese Days*. Thought it was non-fiction; turns out to be a novel set during the Raj. I prefer novels. Read for two hours, then tea. In the washroom, there's a man with an Air Canada flight bag. We start to chat and I join him at the poolside. Black bikinis are in, here.

My new friend's from Calgary. Working in Pakistan for six months for a hundred dollars per day plus accommodation. Not great, he says; others get two or three hundred. Says I might have made a mistake drinking that glass of water at the airport. Thanks a lot. Force myself to relax. Now I know why the British had their clubs. Outside there's heat, dust, dirt, and women begging. Here there's water, shade, and pink bougainvillea. I ask about all the soldiers at the airport. He says election day is two weeks from now. The entire European community knows it should stay home because there will be violence. Under Bhutto's regime, the oilman says, the men who served here at the pool made 2,000 rupees every day and split it six ways. Now, under General Zia's martial law and return to Muslim orthodoxy, the men take in only a few hundred, still split six ways.

Time to leave. I get my luggage.

"What shall I tell Mr. Arnold Brown?" the clerk asks.

Oh, yes.

"Tell him his friend from Canada will be in Bombay and he can call me there."

"But where shall I tell him to call you?"

"He knows where I always stay."

This time the cab driver asks for only thirty rupees. A deal. When we reach the airport, the meter shows fifteen.

A porter takes my luggage before I can stop him. Pushes his way through onlookers. Maybe it's recreation here: all these people at the airport pass their time by watching foreigners come and go. Inside: madness. No queuing at the check-in counter; people press forward, try to shove their tickets into the official's hand, luggage onto the scales. I shove with the rest. An old woman waves her umbrella in frustration. She's getting nowhere, always elbowed aside. Hampered by my suitcase, I'm making little progress.

A second official seems to have an easier time than the first: only four or five in his queue, and it's orderly. I join that one. A boy with a trunk hesitates to look for his father. I take the boy's place. Check in at last, immigration no problem, then another wait at security. There's more than one official at this counter, too, so I take advantage of someone else's hesitation. Am getting good at this. My western upbringing.

The PIA plane is darkly cool, quiet and welcoming. How safe it feels in here.

A Most Honest Engineer

JUST AS CHRISTIANITY has its Trinity of the Father, Son and Holy Ghost, Hinduism has its Triad. Brahma is the Creator, Vishnu the Preserver, and Shiva the Destroyer. If evil gains the upper hand over good, Vishnu comes to earth as an avatar, or incarnation, not to banish evil but to restore the balance between. Vishnu has ten avatars. The eighth was Lord Krishna, who came to earth to kill a demon-king. Krishna is called the Divine One and his name means "Dark" or "Black".

My father's father, B. Krishna-Rao, was nothing like Lord Krishna. And yet, like the lord who played a mythic role in Hinduism, my grandfather played his own legendary, even mythic role in the story of my family. He came to be called the most honest engineer in South India. This happened by chance, another familiar twist of fate, like my great-grandfather losing his land.

As a child, Lord Krishna was fond of pranks. He would upset milk pails and blame other children. As a youth, he dallied with young women. Once, while a group of *gopis* – cowgirls – bathed in a river, he stole their clothes and hid in a tree. He made the *gopis* approach naked, then promised that he would dance with each of them under the autumn moon.

Not only did he keep his promise but he also used his powers to make each *gopi* believe that he danced with her alone. His favourite was Radha, and the Radha-Krishna myth has come to symbolize God's relationship with humans. God dallies with us and leaves when duty calls. We can never predict His return; we can only remain faithful.

After many fierce battles, Lord Krishna kills the demon-king and restores the rightful king to his throne. Tired of fighting, Krishna marries a princess. They have fallen in love at first sight because she is an incarnation of Vishnu's own wife, Lakshmi, the goddess of wealth, and she ensures that Krishna remains a model husband.

Although he longs for peace, the Divine One can not end his battle with evil. He finds himself drawn into a civil war described in the Hindu epic *Mahabharata*. He takes no part in the fighting but he does affect events by giving the advice now found in the *Bhagavad Gita*, also called the *Song of the Lord*. In painting and sculpture, the best-known image from the *Gita* shows Krishna as the charioteer of the great warrior Arjuna. Angry at having to fight his cousins, Arjuna throws down his weapons. Krishna explains that all is *maya*, illusion, even war and death in battle. Men must follow and not question their *dharma*, or sacred duty. They must leave the greater plans to the gods.

After my widowed great-grandmother, Ammiah, moved her daughter and my grandfather Krishna to Bangalore, she insisted that he attend secondary school. The Brahmin principal of his school gave him a letter saying that he was a student in good standing and deserved help from fellow Brahmins – members of the highest caste in the Hindu hierarchy. On each day of the week, Krishna took home food from a different Brahmin household. In this way he fed Ammiah, his sister and himself until he earned his SSLC, his

Secondary School Leaving Certificate.

He seems not to have had much of a childhood or youth. I doubt that he upset milk pails; he certainly never dallied with cowgirls. He attended college on a scholarship and became a civil engineer. Meanwhile, Ammiah arranged her daughter's marriage to a young lawyer. He may have been only a pleader, someone who petitions judges on behalf of clients but has less status than a barrister. Whatever the case, he was glad to marry the sister of an educated man.

One day, Krishna and Ammiah went to a wedding. Everyone was waiting for the groom's family to arrive but a telegram arrived instead. There had been a death in the groom's family. Could the wedding be postponed? The bride's parents grew annoyed. They had hired the priests and musicians and ordered food for the wedding party and their guests. Rather than see these preparations wasted, the parents decided that Krishna would be a suitable boy for their daughter. I don't know the name of this wife, his first, and there is no need to invent one for her because I've never heard a story about her. She did leave her mark on the family, though, by bearing Krishna two daughters and a son.

I knew the daughters, my aunts Mani and Ratna, when I lived in India as a boy. I met the son, my Uncle Chaitanya, during my first visit back. There was also another son – a nephew, actually – who was orphaned while still quite young and adopted by Krishna and his first wife. This was my Uncle Nagasha. He lived in Mysore in Beegamudre House. He was an engineer as well, and I met him during my 1977–78 trip.

After his first wife died, Krishna married again – to the young woman who would become my grandmother.

For a while, Krishna lived in obscurity as a junior civil servant for Mysore State. The maharajah of the day was determined to develop the state's resources. Among them were its rivers, natural sources of power. India's first hydroelectric station had been built in 1902 east of Mysore City at Shivasamudram, by an engineer who, later, might or might not have become Krishna's mentor. Let us say he did. Krishna began his career by surveying more sites for dams and power stations. He spent weeks in jungle-covered hills accompanied by bearers and a guide. The guide carried a gun because tigers still roamed the hills.

Later, Krishna became the manager of a huge irrigation system in the hills. It worked simply but carried a danger. A series of tanks, artificial ponds walled with concrete, had been built along a slope to store water that fell during the monsoons. After one tank filled, water flowed into a lower tank; after this one filled, the water flowed into an even lower tank. Shortly after Krishna became managing engineer of the system, torrential rains fell. The gates controlling the flow of water gave way, and water swept uncontrolled down the hillside. It must have seemed like a tidal wave. Hundreds of villagers drowned.

Krishna found himself the central figure of an inquiry. Another man might have used his influence to escape investigation but Krishna was not well connected. Besides, he'd done nothing wrong. If he was like me, he was not a forgiving man. Coolly, perhaps even coldly, he proved his innocence. He described how he would have built the system: how thick and deep the foundations should have been; what machinery he would have installed to control the flow of water. He showed that had the system been built to even minimum standards, it would not have failed. He was cleared, and the engineers who had built the system were charged. Overnight, he earned the label that stayed with him throughout his career: the most honest engineer in South India.

He impressed his superiors with methodical work and his refusal to let ambition sway his judgment. Honesty may have had little to do with this, but in a country notorious for dishonesty and casual standards, he must have seemed like a godsend. No doubt even his superiors regarded him as odd. Any civil servant who refused to curry and dispense favours surely couldn't be trusted, but Krishna's superiors used him well.

He seems to have built his reputation on hills. He had little use for politics, even avoiding the growing nationalist movement, but he wasn't afraid of Englishmen. One was an engineer named Welltrap. Armed with surveying equipment, Krishna visited a dam site being constructed by this Welltrap. His Indian subordinates already knew of Krishna's reputation as incorruptible. No doubt they shunned him and called him a spy for desk-bound officials who rarely ventured into the field. If any of this bothered him, he refused to let it show. He set about comparing reports on the construction's progress with his own observations. He estimated how much earth had been excavated from the side of the hill by the men on the site, then compared his estimates with the payments made to the contractors. The discrepancies were huge. The contractors had clearly been submitting figures that inflated the amount of work actually done.

If this were a novel, I could describe Welltrap's subordinates' plotting to get rid of Krishna, or at least discredit him, to protect the bribes they had received. None of this was necessary in real life. One day, towards the end of his investigation, he crossed the temporary dam, built to keep back water while the permanent dam was built downstream. Welltrap strode toward him and they met in the middle.

"Mr. Krishna-Rao," Welltrap said, "if you submit your report, I shall ensure you will be broken to the bottom of your service."

"Mr. Welltrap," Krishna said, "if that happens, I shall take you with me."

He filed his report. The Indian engineers and contractors were charged with fraud but, because Welltrap was an Englishman, he was allowed to find employment elsewhere. During the thirty-five years of Krishna's service, from about 1910 to 1945, he worked his way steadily up towards the post of chief engineer for the state. He never reached it but in his early fifties he did became one of the state's two superintending engineers. Each was responsible for projects in half of the state. Ammiah watched all this and approved – of most of it. Part of Krishna's stipend included a car and driver. He lived close to his office, in Mysore City, and planned to walk to work each morning, but Ammiah would not let him. "I've waited so long to see this happen that you won't disappoint me," she said. "I want to see you get into that motor car in the morning and be driven to your office. At night, when you come home, I want to see you step out of that motor car."

Krishna obeyed her, as everyone did. When he finally retired, in his mid-fifties, he retired a year early so that one of his friends, a former classmate, could also retire on the pension of a superintending engineer.

The only recognition I have seen of Krishna's work is a sky blue woollen shawl that he received towards the end of his service. In the maharajah's *diwan*, or audience hall, Krishna waited to be announced. Then he walked along a carpet towards the maharajah, who sat on his throne. After the chief minister read a list of Krishna's accomplishments, the maharajah handed Krishna the sky blue shawl. It was embroidered with mango leaves, what we sometimes call paisley. It would be tempting to say that the embroidery was gold, but it wasn't – it was yellow silk.

After Krishna left the Public Works Department, he worked for another ten years as a consultant to various South Indian states. By now, he was taking more interest in his family. His first three children were grown and married. My grandmother's children, my father and his brother, were approaching their teens. Krishna found time for them – something that he'd rarely had for his first three children, even though his second marriage was not a happy one. He'd become set in his ways and even seemed to enjoy playing the eccentric. Once, my grandmother sent him to the railway station to meet relatives who were arriving for a wedding. Instead of taking his car and driver and perhaps hiring an extra cab or two, Krishna hired a truck and made the guests sit on benches in the back. Then he had the driver speed through the streets. The guests, dressed in their finery, clung to the benches when the truck rounded corners. At the wedding hall Krishna said, "I trust all of you had a pleasant journey?"

Often his eccentricity overshadowed his generosity. He had succeeded because of his education, even if his family no longer had its land. He announced that as long as his nieces and nephews remained in school, he would support them. Support meant tuition, room and board. Room meant a place on his verandah for a bedroll. My father slept on this verandah when he came home from boarding school. Sometimes half a dozen children slept on that veranda. To keep order, Krishna drew lines with chalk. Even while sleeping, no one was allowed to cross those lines. Krishna rose early. If he saw an arm or a leg across a chalk mark, he tapped the offending limb with his walking stick.

He was not an overly religious man – he was certainly the most modern man my family had seen to date – and sometimes he apparently forgot his Hindu legacy entirely.

One of our ancestors was a saint named Raghavendra Swami. He was a poor villager but one day he had a vision and left his wife and young son. Raghavendra fasted and prayed and studied until he became a holy man. He became renowned for his powers of healing, though these were incidental to his intellectual and spiritual powers. When Hindus die, they are buried only if they are infants or holy men. All other Hindus are cremated in order to free their souls. Infants are not cremated because they haven't had time to develop souls. Holy men aren't cremated because they are so enlightened that they don't need fire to free their souls. When the time came for Raghavendra to die, he told his disciples to seal his body into a cave. First he went into a trance. He slowed his breathing till his pulse became almost imperceptible. Then his disciples sealed the mouth of the cave with slabs of stone. And so, according to legend, he never died.

One day Krishna cut himself badly while shaving and the wound refused to heal. He tried allopathy, the term given to western medicine. He tried ayurveda, which uses herbs to correct imbalances in bodily functions. He tried homeopathy, a German form of medicine that he taught himself and later practised on my father. Nothing worked. Then someone reminded Krishna of Raghavendra Swami. Krishna went to the holy place – called Mantralayam, the Place of Song – and performed all the proper rites. These included bathing in the nearby river and circling the shrine, repeating prayers and even feeding the poor. The wound healed. I never completely believed this story until I saw a picture of Raghavendra during my first India trip. The picture hung in the cafeteria of Mysore Medical College.

My own memories of Krishna are of an old man. He must have been seventy when I was a child in India. He'd built a house in an outlying district of Bangalore called Jayanagar and refused to have anything to do with his family. "I have helped all of you through your troubles," he said. "Now leave me in peace."

My mother was raising me alone at the time – alone but for the help of a servant named Mary, a Christian Indian. When I was five, I developed a rash that prevented me from walking and Krishna practised his homeopathy on me with little success. He visited us every Sunday, while Mary and my mother made carrot halva, I waited for his arrival – his weekly return. To me he seemed like a god.

Until recently I didn't own a single photograph of him but I did remember what he looked like. He was short and dark and had stubbly white hair. His nose was large and might have been called beaked if it hadn't been pressed almost flat. He wore glasses, carried an umbrella to protect himself from the sun, and often smacked his lips. He wore a white cotton *dhoti*, a type of loose sarong worn by South Indian men, and a shirt buttoned at the collar. Rather than the sandals worn by many men, he wore heavy black shoes. I remember this because, after he sat in one of the two wicker chairs on our verandah, I untied his laces, took off his shoes, and placed them under the chair. Then I sat on the floor while he and my mother chatted and Mary made their tea.

Perhaps he was kind to me only because I was ill, but I like to think that we had the bond that develops between grandfathers and grandsons. During my second India trip, my cousin Radha – named for Lord Krishna's favourite *gopi* – told me that she used to take me to the house in Jayanagar district. My grandfather would ask her to take me away when he grew tired of my chatter. He was a man to whom affection did not come easily and yet, when my mother and I left India in 1962, he came to the train station without telling us that he would see us off. For years I imagined that he came to an airport but few people, if any, took planes within India then. Besides, we weren't leaving India just yet; we would do that from Bombay Airport. Just before our train left then, not our plane, he handed my mother a paper bag. She opened it after we settled into our compartment. The bag contained pears. Some were too ripe in places, the green skin softening to brown. Nestled among the pears, protected by carefully creased paper, was a new blue safety razor blade, a Gillette for skinning the fruit.

Krishna died shortly afterwards. I don't remember exactly when; only that both he and Jawaharlal Nehru, India's first prime minister, died soon after we joined my father in Canada. They died even as I began forgetting about life in India – forgetting because I was trying so hard to become Canadian. Many years later, in 1983, Richard Attenborough's film *Gandhi* appeared. The children of a friend were watching TV and saw a clip from the film. A Shakespearean actor named Ben Kingsley, then unknown in North America, was playing Gandhi and the children assumed that it was me. My friend and I shared a good laugh; but, when I later told my father about this, he didn't think the incident was ridiculous. He said I had Krishna's jawline; that he had, indeed, sometimes been mistaken for Gandhi. It's difficult to imagine how this could happen, as Gandhi would have been thirty years older than Krishna and the resemblance was, if anything, slight. But given that Gandhi was a legend even when he was alive, and given that legends neither age nor die, the mistake may have been natural.

My father's comment led me to start a long story called "Gandhi Himself." It's about an engineer named Mohandas, which was Gandhi's first name. The story is unfinished because it depends too much on a premise that risks turning into a gag: that the engineer, mistaken for Gandhi, finds himself enchanted by a widowed missionary and leads workers in a strike against landowners. The young widow and the strike both change Mohandas; he becomes less rigid, more forgiving of others' faults. I would like to think that Krishna learned this as well, because it's something I am still learning.

There are many ironies in writing fiction that is based on family stories. It's difficult to separate what really happened in someone's life from what we hear. Who, for instance, told our family about the encounter with Welltrap if not Krishna himself? And was he really so fearless – such a master of repartee – or did he create and then have to live up to his own legend? For another thing, spinning tales makes it difficult to separate what we hear from what we later invent because we can't bear gaps. And yet, does this even matter? Sometimes what we invent – or reinvent – rings more true than what little we know about someone. The character of Mohandas is much like Krishna's own character. Even if this were not so, fictionalizing him has kept him alive for me in a way that neither anecdotes nor photographs ever could. Of all the people in my family, Krishna is the one person I would bring back to life if I had this power. I know I would find him annoying but I would like to think that we have much in common. At the very least, unlike the three people who took turns raising me – first my grandmother, then my mother and then my father – my favourite grandfather did nothing that I need to forgive.

If I had a son, I would name him Krishna. No, this is not completely true. If I'm to be honest, I should say this:

Had our son been born, we would have named him Krishna.

[Author's Note: go to "Gandhi Himself" in the Bonus Materials]

THE ONLY WHITE MAN HERE

Saturday, October 1, 1977 (continued)

WE LAND AT BOMBAY'S Santa Cruz Airport – the name Santa Cruz a holdover from the Portuguese colonial period. It's 7:30 p.m. Pakistan Standard Time but 8:00 p.m. here. If I can rush through immigration and customs, I can see about booking an Indian Airlines flight to Bangalore for tomorrow. No such luck. Have spent nearly half an hour at immigration although I started out fourth in line. They're making the first man sweat. Keeps wiping his face with a handkerchief. He's Indian and spent too long in Pakistan for his own good. They scrutinize his documents, make him fill out a long form and explain everything he wrote. The man in front of me is Indian from Vancouver, with a Canadian passport. I show him mine and he grins at our shared special status.

Get my suitcase. A boy keeps following until I shoo him away. Search for the Indian Airlines counter; shuttle between two or three. My Aunt Rama Menon lives in Bombay, but I left her address behind in Ottawa. Waiting for my suitcase, I check the phone directory. There are far too many Menons in Bombay. The first phone doesn't work. The second one does but the woman who answers keeps on shouting, "Hallo?"

I ask the first white man I see why the terminal's almost deserted. Indian Airlines is on strike, he says. All domestic flights have been cancelled. He suggests that I stay at a nearby hotel and take the train to Bangalore. Carries my suitcase for me. He's an Englishman working in India for Brooke Bond's meat division. Seems to know India well. The hotel is across from the airport at the end of a tree-lined lane.

The Centaur Hotel. Even more sumptuous than the Karachi Intercontinental. Modern paintings of women in saris, luxurious lounging areas. Well dressed, well groomed women manning all the posts. The room costs 287 rupees (about thirty-six dollars). A sofa and armchair, large dressing area, plenty of mirrors, bathroom with a real shower, which I use gratefully. Downstairs again, a supper of eggs Florentine and a lime soda. Hostesses in blue and red saris; uniformed waiters. It's all so civilized.

Sunday, October 2, 1977

AM AWAKENED at 9:30 a.m. by the operator. The train to Bangalore has already left from Bombay VT (Victoria Terminus). If I want a ticket for this afternoon's train, I should leave now for Churchgate Station. Taxi into city centre. The main road's like the road from the airport into Karachi but even worse. People live in huts on sidewalks. Blocks of flats look as decayed as ruins. Once, the driver stops for a signal and a woman shoves a "Save a Child" ticket through my open window. Another time, a beggar tries to shove his arm into my face. The arm's amputated at the elbow.

Downtown Bombay is on or near a bay. I get it: Bom-bay. Modern buildings like Air India, Tata Exports with its clean new trucks in showrooms behind plate glass windows. The driver charges me twice what his meter shows. Waves a fare card in my face. I refuse to pay extra for the suitcase. Counter to counter in Churchgate Station, then to a Government of India tourist office. Have to buy the ticket at VT itself; that's where the train leaves from. Another taxi ride, this one shorter, to VT. Houses on the way: little more than abandoned shops opening onto the street. People lie on beds made of benches.

No first-class berths are available till next Thursday, October 6th. Will have to go by second class if I want to go today – hard wooden benches for sleeping. Half an hour after reaching VT, I find the right queue. Am about twentieth in line, behind some friendly young men. One's a South Indian named Kilkurny. He says to bribe my way into getting a first-class ticket. He'll save my place. No luck. The clerk's absolutely white. An albino Indian? Says I can have a berth to Miraj, halfway to Bangalore, with no guarantee of a connection. Tell him I'll be back in half an hour if I want it. He shrugs.

Back in the queue, back to my new friend Kilkurny. He's glad to talk. Under Mrs. Gandhi's emergency legislation, the service sector – civil servants, at least – worked efficiently because jobs were on the line. Did he prefer that to this, now? "Yes," he says. "The common man who can never hope to become rich overnight could not afford to waste so much time securing tickets and so on." Kilkurny works as a sales engineer six days a week. Today's his day off. He took a local train from near his parents' house, where he lives, forty-five minutes outside the city centre. The ticket is for a friend.

At 12:30, the wickets close for a half-hour lunch. What! The clerks all go for lunch at the same time here. As if that's not enough, there's a sign above the wickets, a quote from a speech by Mahatma Gandhi to railway workers:

> A customer is the most important visitor on our premises.
> He is not dependent on us. We are dependent on him. He
> is not an interruption on our work. He is the purpose of
> it. He is not an outsider on our business. He is part of it.
> We are not doing him a favour by serving him. He is doing
> us a favour by giving us the opportunity to do so.

The clerks return. My goal's a barricade starting about six feet from the wicket. Fight the urge to sit down. I'll lean against the barricade once I'm there. At two o'clock I'm still only the eighth person in line. I can taste a lime soda. Kilkurny offers to watch my suitcase again but now I'm stubborn. The queue's even longer than when I started. I count and calculate. At this rate, the people at the end won't reach the wickets before they close at 4:30. "A customer is the most important visitor on our premises."

Kilkurny gets an idea. I've long ago filled in my application for a ticket. The form asks irrelevant questions like age. Twenty-one and glad of it. He tells me to take the form to the Chief Reservations Officer. So I do. Try not to think about whether I should have done this before. The CRO asks me to sit down while he reads the form. Outside the door, my queue friends are grinning.

"You must find it exhausting to work here," I say. Really need to be ironic.

"What can we do?" he asks piously. "There are so many people."

I leave with my ticket. Kilkurny has his and I offer him a drink. He takes me to an outdoor snack bar called Super Snack Bar. It's not really. Have bottled sodas while a Sikh at a nearby table eats chicken. I'm not hungry. Across the road, a theatre's showing *Airport 1975*. Wouldn't mind seeing it.

Kilkurny jumps up and crosses the road. Comes back to say the movie's sold out. New ones usually are. New? It's two years old. He smiles and says, "New for here." We take a cab to the nearest European hotel, the Grand, where we part. I spend the rest of the afternoon here – waiting for Arnold Brown.

Late lunch in the dining room served by two old men in off-white uniforms with blue facings. "I'm the only white man here," I think. Then, in the washroom, I look into the mirror. Other men, all Indians, are using the washroom too and mine's the darkest face in the mirror.

Back in the dining room again, through the window I watch a family working across the street. The husband beats a two-sided drum with sticks. The wife twirls their baby. Shrieks to attract attention each time she tosses the baby into the air. High.

At seven I leave another message for Arnold Brown. Head back to Bombay VT. Fight off porters in red clothes and turbans. Find a quiet bench. Not for long, though. I'm surrounded by a group of quarrelling men after one of them sits down beside me. The Mahalaxmi Express arrives and I find my carriage. It's a three-tiered sleeping car that provides no passage to the cars at either end. I search in the dark for number forty-four above backs of hard wooden seats. Sit alone, feeling rather pleased with myself. Hum the tune "Song of India." Phileas Fogg was here, on his journey around the world in eighty days. So was David Niven in the film. He saved a princess (Shirley MacLaine) from suttee and even married her. Lucky fellow. Jean Passepartout, as in Passport, has a handlebar moustache.

Someone has thrown a cigarette butt from a window into a shrub at the foot of an iron trestle. The shrub bursts into flame. I watch the fire while the carriage fills. Sometime after the fire burns itself out we leave. The line out of Bombay passes factories and slums. Dwellings closest to the track look like cardboard shacks with corrugated tin roofs. Each hut has a fire glowing inside. Once, we pass a local commuter train, the kind Kilkurny would be on now. Has no doors. Hanging onto straps, people stand. There are so many that they don't sway.

My carriage is divided into sections of two seats facing one another. Each seat is wide enough for three people. The seats end at an off-centre aisle. On the other side single seats face one another with a single berth above. Above our seats are two berths. People have brought bedrolls or sheets to lie on. I never thought of this.

I talk with the head of a small family that shares my section with me. His wife doesn't talk; feeds their baby with a bottle. He's a boy of six months with bracelets on his wrists and earrings in his small lobes. She plays with the baby by slapping him. Hard. The husband asks about Canada. Gives me a cigarette during a brief stop. Asks if I'm married. Why? Do I look as though I should be married? Likely would be by now if I'd stayed in India. Imagine that: a householder at twenty-one.

Later, after the lights go out, I can't sleep because now his wife chatters. I move away to another berth. Noise of wheels loud through the open windows. Headlights of large vehicles – trucks? lorries? – curve down towards the track at crossings. Need a bath because my skin feels dry but I resist scratching. Well after midnight, I finally fall asleep.

Monday, October 3, 1977

ONE LONG TRAIN RIDE. Wake at 3:00 a.m. at a station. Tea vendors crying, *"Chai! chai!"* Can't fall asleep again. There's so much noise: train wheels, baby cries, a fat blubbery woman coughing on the berth above.

Towards dawn, a man sits down at the end of my berth and we chat. He works for Colgate-Palmolive in New Delhi. He visited one of his sons in Bombay and is travelling with his second son to this one's home in Bangalore. Father and son are both tall and the son has fair skin like my cousin Prakash Burra. Also a half beard. Speaks good English and could pass for a westerner. At five, the rest of the men wake and dress. The father's wearing a dhoti. He changes into trousers by using his dhoti as a screen, holding two corners in his teeth. Using my towel, I change my underwear.

Go to the latrine. An old man's being helped out. He's so thin that I could make a ring with my thumb and middle finger around his elbow. The latrine's a hole in an aluminum pan set in the floor. Two raised footrests, both of them dirty and wet.

Miraj Junction. The father and son help me change trains. We leave our broad-gauged train, pulled by a diesel, to a smaller, metre-gauged train. The son brings me breakfast: half a bun, two cups of tea, two bananas. Besides express trains like ours, there are mail-passenger trains with steam engines; wooden carriages instead of metal. These can take eight hours to cover 125 miles. We sit in a reserved car. This means nothing more than having your name against each seat number on the conductor's list. The conductor is middle-aged. Has a badge pinned on his dark coat. His real badge of rank is his small vinyl briefcase.

Sharing two wooden seats, which face one another, are a woman with a young man and two other young men. She wears a blue sari and never speaks. He sleeps on the seat with his knees drawn up or with his feet blocking the aisle, which runs the length of one side of the car. The two young men sleep on one another – one resting his head on the other's knee, the second hunched over his friend's back. They look so much more relaxed than the rest of us. In the car is also a huge, fat man, the husband of the woman who coughed all night. He wears a T-shirt and dhoti and gets down at every station with a silver pot for new drinking water.

The countryside: variations on the same theme. The land is almost all cultivated with maize that grows tall in fields; rice grows less than a foot above the surface of paddies. Farther south, the soil's a reddish brown. The water in rivers and irrigation ditches is orange instead of yellow-brown as it was farther north. Black water buffalo wade with only their heads above the surface and look like black crocodiles, hunting for prey. A few peasants work their fields. Most seem to be simply walking from one place to another. The land near Bangalore is rocky. Lots of hills with boulders. Sky filled with clouds but not really overcast. Huge clouds, thick and white like clotted cream, they hover without menacing. We pass through a shower, then see three rainbows, one after the other. I take a picture. Am still rationing my film. Nothing much to see, anyway.

Stations all look the same. Tea vendors wash their glasses out with half cups of water. Coffee vendors. Fruit, peanut, and prepared-food sellers. These yell, "*Idli! Wada!*" Also at every station: dogs. None of them fat. Sometimes goats chewing banana peels. Once, an ugly black pig.

Only one real beggar: a blind man feels his way onto our carriage, plays on a stringed instrument till the next stop. Then he goes along with his hand outstretched. Keeps it under my nose for half a minute but I don't look up. Am making yesterday's entry with my pen – my stainless steel Parker 45.

Children at every station: boys and girls dressed in rags but not emaciated, as I'd expected. Stand at a window without moving and with hands out. Call, *"Baba! Baba!"* I learn to shoo the children off with a backwards wave of the hand. Feel sorry only once, for an old man in another carriage. His right leg is swollen three times larger than his left. Elephantiasis. Looks grotesque even under the almost clean cloth wrappings.

At one station I copy down the sign outside a vegetarian refreshment room:

> No admission to destitutes, urchins,
> invalids, and lepers. By order.

I can sit on my folded towel for less and less time now. Take to standing in the open door of the carriage. Hang onto two bars and watch the countryside whiz by. Sunflowers. Palms planted evenly in rows. Trees that might be acacias. Huge, blue plants like the tops of pineapples. Seems villagers beat this plant into string used in table mats. On the calm surface of one yellow river: a water snake.

Bangalore at last, a disappointment. I expected it to be different from Bombay. Here there's still the noise of automobiles, black and yellow autorickshaws like weaving bumblebees, buses – all of them honking their horns nonstop. Many streets not paved. Animals everywhere.

REUNIONS AT THE PINK HOUSE

My maternal great-grandfather, C.S.R. Rao, who wrote as the Jack of Spades,
shortly after he was made a Rao Sahib for his contributions to imperial journalism.

1

MY GRANDMOTHER'S HOUSE has two gates. The iron from
which they were wrought long ago turned to irony. On one
gate is my uncle's name, ANANDA, after whom she also
named the house. He was the younger of her two sons, and
he rewarded her faith in him by becoming not only a fine
engineer but also vice-president of a bank. On the other

gate is my last name. She made a point of telling me it was mine, not my father's; that, although he may also have become a fine engineer, he confirmed her lack of faith in him by remaining penniless. There's another difference between the gates: while the one marked ANANDA leads to her front door, the one marked BEGAMUDRE leads to a driveway. This, in turn, leads to a garage. Since she has never owned a car, she rents the garage out as living quarters to college students who can't find what Indians call preferred accommodation.

WHEN MY WIDOWED GRANDFATHER Krishna remarried in 1925, he was in his late thirties. His bride was fifteen. It's unlikely she considered herself a second mother to the four children from his first marriage, since the elder of his two daughters was nearly her age and the youngest boy was barely ten years younger than her. The girls, especially, regarded her as an interloper. She considered them irritants. Which came first is hard to say and it didn't matter because the children attended boarding schools.

Krishna was too old for his bride; she soon considered herself too good for him. His father had been a farmer and village headman, hers a journalist. Her mother had died young, and the widowed journalist had lavished both money and attention on his daughter before finding her a promising match. After he retired, he wrote a bridge column under the pseudonym Jack of Spades. By then he'd been made a Rao Sahib, an imperial distinction somewhat short of a knighthood.

Much later in the life of Krishna's second wife, her calling card would read,

Smt. B. Bhagirathi-Bai

Smt. is short for Shrimati, a respectful designation, just as
Mrs. is short for Mistress. Like my grandfather Krishna, Bhagirathi was also named for a Hindu deity: he for a god who
came to earth as a cowherd, she for a goddess who came to
earth as a river. The card continues,

MA, BT, Mont. Dip., MA, PD (Columbia)
Educationist and Social Worker
Rtd. Lecturer in Education
Ex-Principal, Mauritius

Bhagirathi had no intention of remaining at home while
Krishna pursued his career. She bore him two sons within
three years of the marriage: first my father in 1926; then, a
year and a half later, my Uncle Ananda. She continued her
schooling and, by the mid-1930s, graduated from teachers'
college. She had plenty of time to pursue her career because
she sent both boys to boarding school. She sent Ananda only
because he wanted to be with my father. She sent my father
because – and this was according to my own mother – Bhagirathi wanted to be rid of him.

Although remarried, Krishna had continued building his
power stations and inspecting dams. Meanwhile, Bhagirathi
had made friends with a classmate who occasionally called
at the house. One day, while Krishna was home on leave, my
father inadvertently mentioned this new "uncle." Krishna
became furious. He ordered her not to entertain men who
were not relatives and so – again, according to my mother –
Bhagirathi took revenge on my father by packing him off to
school. On the one hand, it rid her of him and denied him
Krishna's presence during leaves. On the other hand, it
nearly placed Ananda beyond her reach – especially when,
some years later, he joined the merchant marine. No matter;
he remained her favourite. She helped him buy a flat on

Bombay's Malabar Hill: posh yet not nearly as posh as the house he later bought in Geneva, a continent away.

When Bhagirathi's sons were in their twenties – one of them in college, the other at sea – she went all the way to New York to study education at Columbia. She would have been in her early forties. By the time I was born, shortly afterward, she was living in Mauritius. This was where my parents left me – with her – on their way to separate American graduate schools.

Mauritius is one of the Mascarene Islands of the Indian Ocean. The others are Réunion and Rodrigues. They lie east of Madagascar and just north of the Tropic of Capricorn and are collectively named for the Portuguese explorer Pedro Mascarenhas. Colonized by the French in 1721, Mauritius was captured by the British in 1810 and remained their colony until 1968. Its population is Indian, Creole, European, Malagasy and Chinese. Bhagirathi would remain fond of the island. Her time there, as principal of a Montessori school, may have been the best years of her life. During my first India trip, in 1977–78, she offered to pay my way to Mauritius if I would write a book about it. I declined. I wanted to write novels, after all; not travel books.

I spent a year and a half with her as a toddler in Mauritius during the late 1950s. I remember little about our time there, but I have many of the photographs she took. In one, I'm on the hood of a car next to the neighbour who likely owned it. In another, I'm in a tropical canoe; moss garlands trees beyond the beach. Two other photos were posed in studios. In the first, taken shortly after my arrival, I'm a year and a half. In the other, taken shortly before my departure, I've celebrated my third birthday. In this portrait, I stand on a box next to her, in a tropical sailor suit: whites. The first portrait, the one in which she holds me, draws the eye back. Behind us a footbridge arcs over a stream; beyond this the branches of European trees emerge from a foreign mist. She looks determined. She also appears to be suppressing a smile. I think she gave me much of the love she couldn't give her own sons – especially the first, born while she'd been too young. Thirty years later he gave her a grandson she could mother.

My earliest memory is from those Mauritius days. We're riding in a car past a pond full of ducks – my grandmother, my mother and I.

2

SAGARA, KING OF AYODHYA, had two wives but no sons. In return for Sagara's austerities, Lord Shiva – a member of the omnipotent Hindu Triad – announced that one of the wives would bear sixty thousand sons and the other would bear only one. However, he added, the sixty thousand would perish while the one would continue Sagara's line. This one son grew to be immoral, but his son – Sagara's grandson, Ansuman – proved both valiant and wise. The princes also grew up valiant but they proved to be thoughtless. And so the gods decided to teach them a lesson.

One day, while Sagara performed a ritual horse sacrifice to extend the borders of his kingdom, the god of the firmament stole the sacrificial horse. Sagara ordered the princes to regain it. After searching the entire world, they decided to search the nether world. Each prince dug one league. Even after they had dug sixty thousand leagues, they could not find the horse. Meanwhile, Earth complained to the gods about the deep crater in her side. At last, the princes found the horse in the garden of a sage who sat in meditation. They called him a thief. He, in turn, uttered a single powerful syllable that burnt them to ashes. When the princes did not return, Sagara sent his wise grandson, Ansuman, to find them. He found only the sage, who was impressed by his humility and agreed that he could take the horse back to Ayodhya. The sage also revealed that the princes' ashes could be purified only if the sacred waters of the Ganga River could be brought to earth.

Ganga was the beautiful daughter of Mount Himavan, god of the Himalayas. She could purify anything she touched. She was also strong-willed.

Although Sagara reigned for thirty thousand years, he died without bringing Ganga to earth. His wise grandson, Ansuman, also tried. So did his son; yet neither of them succeeded. And so the task fell to Ansuman's grandson, Bhagiratha. Bhagiratha swore he would refuse his crown until the task was done. He lived in the forest for years. He underwent austerities and meditated until finally Lord Brahma, also a member of the omnipotent Triad, agreed to allow Ganga to flow to earth. However, he warned Bhagiratha that Ganga was unwilling to leave heaven; that if she did come to earth, she would fall as heavily as she could. Bhagiratha underwent even more austerities, this time to please Lord Shiva. Shiva agreed to stand on a Himalayan mountain and break Ganga's fall by catching her in his matted hair. So Ganga fell. She had planned to sweep the earth into the nether world, but she became confused in Shiva's locks. She emerged as seven separate streams. One became what we call the Ganges; what many Indians call the Ganga. This sacred stream followed Bhagiratha's chariot, and he led her toward the nether world.

Along the way, Ganga mischievously flooded the garden of yet another sage. His sacrificial fire went out. In his anger he swallowed the stream, then agreed to release it so that Bhagiratha's austerities would not go unrewarded. From her

contact with this sage, Ganga became even more pure. She
flowed into the crater in Earth's side and created the oceans;
what many Indians call Sagara. Earth sighed. Ganga flowed
into the nether world. With their ashes purified at last, the
princes' souls entered heaven. Bhagiratha accepted his
crown. At the coronation, Brahma announced that, since
Bhagiratha had brought Ganga to earth, she would also be
called Bhagirathi: Daughter of Bhagiratha.

MY GRANDMOTHER Bhagirathi couldn't keep my Uncle Ananda
with her for long, so she tried to keep me instead. My mother
was easily betrayed by her emotions. Bhagirathi knew this.
Even as my mother finished her studies in America, Bhagirathi wrote, "You are not fit to raise the boy." There was some
truth in this. My mother knew little about keeping house
and even less about raising children, since her family's servants had done such things. But though she had been spoiled
and was unaccountably prone to despair, she fought back.
She appealed to the Bishop of Mauritius to intervene, and he
did. He wrote a letter saying that no one should separate a
son from his mother. Armed with this letter, my mother flew
from America to Mauritius to reclaim me. Like the story of
how my father entered boarding school, this story was also
according to my mother. I have no way of knowing whether
it's true. I have no real interest in finding out. I could ask my
relatives for the truth as they know it, but some questions
are best left unasked. Just as some gates are best left closed.

LESS THAN A YEAR after my mother returned to India with me
and we settled in my hometown of Bangalore, I turned four.
My mother ordered a birthday cake complete with icing and

candles. Somewhere in a box or a file there's a photo of me with this cake.

Bhagirathi retired that spring to her house in Malleswaram, the part of Bangalore we consider our home district. Her house was on Margosa Road, a commercial thoroughfare running north-south from Tumkur Road near Play Ground to 5th Cross Road near K.C. General Hospital. She lived upstairs and rented the ground floor to a maker of musical instruments. Margosa Road was named for the margosa trees that lined it – those trees of the bitter, medicinal sap. There was one of these trees directly in front of her house until a truck ran into it and it had to be removed.

Sometimes my mother allowed me to visit Bhagirathi; sometimes my mother refused. It depended on whether they were speaking. The only meal I recall eating in the house on Margosa Road was one that I ate there with my father. This was during his visit to India, one that made little impression on me because he didn't stay with us. He stayed with Bhagirathi. Her servant made *dosas*, or pancakes, and Bhagirathi allowed me to watch while she herself made baby pancakes. My mother called Bhagirathi stingy; my father later said she considered herself too good for my grandfather, who had long ago retired to a different part of Bangalore. My father meant she wasn't good enough to be a Begamudré, which was also what Bhagirathi thought of my mother.

And I? Picture me living in a dream world of birthday cakes, *dosas* and women who competed for my love. Picture me as an Indian prince.

3

THE FALL AFTER I turned twelve, Bhagirathi came to Kingston, Ontario, to spend a year with us; with my father and me. He was teaching at the Royal Military College. She may not have had much love for him but she did love me. She was supposed to have visited us the year before, but she'd broken her hip in a fall and the fracture had taken months to heal. She would have been in her late fifties now. I had little time for her. When I wasn't at school, I took refuge in homework or in long novels. On holidays I sat in the dining room and built model ships – the HMS *Victory*, the USS *Constitution* – while she watched soap operas on our black and white TV. I couldn't abide soap operas. My mother also watched them and, when I visited her in Toronto, she would tell me about a character named Rachel who was forever scheming.

At times Bhagirathi became fed up with the quarrelling on screen. "Too much fighting!" she exclaimed. "Too much fighting!"

Exasperated, I asked, "Why do you watch, then?"

"I want to learn how people live here," she said.

Other times she went for slow, limping walks in her fur coat. My Uncle Ananda had bought it for her because winter in Canada could be cold. He understood winters; he lived in Switzerland. From these walks she often brought back a box of biscuits or wafers. Then I made tea and acted sociable. Sometimes she spent the afternoon making chocolate *halva*, a fudge-like sweet. She was not really making sweets, though; she was making overtures. I accepted the sweets and rejected the overtures. I especially dreaded being seen alone with her in public. She was shorter than I'd remembered; she wore saris that flapped in the wind; she moved her dentures in a mouth that looked simian. Because of her visit, many Indian families invited us for dinner and, at such times, I was glad my father was with us. I could pretend she was his responsibility. I took my cue from him: he, too, avoided her as much as he could by taking refuge in his lab, where he was experimenting with electrical transmission.

One day she did something I could finally appreciate. Our English class often performed scenes from plays. We used no props and improvised costumes. She sewed the yellow stockings with purple cross-garters that I wore as Malvolio in act three, scene four of *Twelfth Night*. I appreciated her gesture because, for once, she didn't try so hard to please. And because it was the closest thing to having a mother in the house. This was one more thing she could hold against my father. "Ananda and his wife live under the same roof," Bhagirathi said. "They live in a proper house, not an apartment house. This is what happens to a man who marries a silly girl who is unfit to raise a child." Then my father grew irritable. He criticized the way she cooked rice or washed dishes. Our apartment felt as small then as it had when my mother lived with us. She hadn't known how to cook rice either. And now, as then, I stayed out of the way. It especially irked me, though I didn't see it till later: my father and his mother quarrelled like a husband and wife.

THE YEAR I TURNED twenty-one, 1977, I returned to India for my first visit. I was ready to be a grandson again. By now Bhagirathi had built a new, two-storey house. It was pink. She lived downstairs because of her limp, and she rented the second floor to Sindhis from North India. For a while she even rented out the garage. This was the house with two gates, the house called ANANDA. I thought of it as the Pink House. I spent many days there during my first India trip, but we rarely talked about people in our family. I couldn't ask her why my father had really gone to boarding school any more than I could ask whether she'd really tried to keep me with her in Mauritius. Instead of answering unasked questions, she did other things for me – small things that even then held significance:

She showed me a blue shawl with yellow embroidery – the shawl presented, some thirty years before, to my grandfather Krishna by the Maharaja of Mysore. The shawl was now moth-eaten. In trying to mend it by cutting and sewing, she'd unwittingly ruined all she had left of her husband, who had been dead for more than a decade.

She showed me a *veena*, a stringed instrument rather like a sitar. After the tree in front of her house on Margosa Road had been toppled by the truck, she had claimed the heartwood and taken it to the downstairs tenant, the maker of musical instruments. I tried playing film songs by ear on that *veena*: "Edelweiss" from *The Sound of Music*, "Somewhere My Love" from *Doctor Zhivago*.

She came looking for me the afternoon my mother suddenly died. I was at a movie, Cecil B. DeMille's *The Ten Commandments*.

$$\rightarrow\!\!\!*\!\!\!\leftarrow$$

THE PINK HOUSE is on a side street off Kumara Krupa Road, which runs southwest to northeast, from Racecourse Road all the way past the Bangalore Golf Club. This part of the city is called High Ground, but the Pink House is closer to the racecourse than to the golf course. Bhagirathi's subdivision is called Kumarcot Layout. She prefers using the more prestigious Kumara Krupa Road as her address, and the post office humours her.

When my father told her to use the correct return address, she would say, "What is there?" as in, "What harm is there?" He too was back in India – teaching at the National Institute of Engineering in Mysore – and we held a brief reunion to mark my twenty-second birthday just before I returned to Canada. Just before I left for home. She'd bought a pound cake filled with cherries. She'd wanted a proper birthday cake complete with icing and candles but hadn't thought to order it in time. My father scoffed at her for putting on airs. She reminded him that her father had been a journalist, a Rao Sahib. They looked for any excuse to quarrel: even birthday cakes.

Ten years later I returned to India once more, this time with my fiancée, Shelley. Besides my father and my mother's twin sister, Shelley had met none of my relatives. She was meeting many of them now. It was her first India trip. Bhagirathi rambled on about relatives and pointed out pictures. One, carefully framed, had been cut from a calendar. It was of Switzerland, where my Uncle Ananda had lived until his premature death nearly a decade before, just short of his fifty-second birthday. My father, now sixty-two, sat in a chair in front of the photograph, directly beneath the western end of Lake Geneva with its mountains, its fountain. He sat wrapped in a plain, unembroidered shawl.

"There," Bhagirathi told Shelley. "My son lives there."

She was now seventy-eight. She'd spent sixty years driven by her feelings for her sons: the favourite, who'd always lived at some distance, and the less favourite, who she'd seen all too often in recent years. Still, I missed the significance of what happened next until Shelley mentioned it later. My father had taken to laughing strangely as he approached his own old age – a half sneer, half leer – just as he did now while Bhagirathi and Shelley were looking at the picture and my own thoughts, as usual, were elsewhere. "What son?" he asked, idly we thought. "Your son is dead."

Taking Baby Jesus

Tuesday, October 4, 1977

GRANDMA'S GARAGE IS RENTED by two students, the upstairs of the house by a family. Downstairs there is a front room with open trellissed windows, a living room with a ceiling fan, a kitchen, two bedrooms with a connecting bathroom (sink and western-style toilet), and a plain Indian-style bathing room, complete with a bucket for water and a brass pot. Last night we tied a mosquito net over my bed. Sounds of children crying and traffic on the road. My skin was dry and I scratched before falling asleep. Didn't awake till noon today. In the afternoon I do little except finish Orwell's *Burmese Days*. Eyes hurt from standing in the train doorway facing the wind.

By phone, Grandma locates an old gentleman named Ramumama. He was a good friend to Mom and me when we lived here. He'll see me this evening at my Uncle Joga-Rao's – my mother's eldest brother.

When I lived in India as a child, my mother used to take me to Ramumama's house. He and his wife were as old as my grandparents, Krishna and Bhagirathi, but, unlike them, Ramumama and his wife lived under the same roof. They were Hindu like us, which meant they also had room in their house for Christianity. Once, while my mother chatted with

58

him in the sitting room, his wife showed me a plastic statue on a low table in a bedroom.

"This is the Christian god's wife," she said. "Her name is Mary, just like your *ayah* (our servant). And this is the son of the Christian god." Ramumama's wife took the son from his mother's lap. He was pink, plastic and naked. "See, Babu? He comes out. His name is Baby Jesus."

I held him in my palm. He was like a doll. She didn't tell me the name of the Christian god or where he was, and I didn't think to ask. I must have been about five.

She put Baby Jesus back in Mary's lap and took my hand. "Time for tea. How many sweets do you want?"

While we ate, I kept remembering Baby Jesus and, after we finished, I wandered away. The adults likely thought I was outside but I wasn't. Later, at home, my mother found me playing with a tiny doll: pink, plastic and naked. "Where did you get that?" she asked.

"It is Baby Jesus," I said. "His *amma's* name is Mary just like our *ayah*. Ramumama Auntie said–"

My mother grasped my hand and we walked all the way back to Ramumama's house. It was near my school, which wasn't far from our own house, but it seemed far. I don't remember her scolding me beyond saying, "Don't take things that aren't yours." She rarely scolded.

Ramumama and his wife insisted that I keep the tiny doll. I put it in my pocket. My mother insisted they have it back.

"All right," Ramumama's wife said. "Do you know where it goes, Babu?"

The adults followed me into the bedroom and I put Baby Jesus back in his mother's lap.

"Doesn't he look happier now?" my mother said.

"Where is his *appa*?" I finally asked. "Where is the Christian god?"

Ramumama's wife said, "He is everywhere," but I didn't understand.

"Where is your *appa*?" Ramumama asked.

"He is studying in America," I said. This is what my mother said whenever I asked about my father. The way she said it, it seemed only natural.

"Correct," Ramumama said. "The Christian god is also studying in America."

GRANDMA AND I take an autorickshaw to Malleswaram, the district where many of Grandma's friends still live. On the way, she argues with the driver for taking a slightly longer route than necessary. I notice little besides traffic noise and smog. Grandma has some business at a bank and I wait. A middle-aged woman named Sushila introduces herself as one of Mom's contemporaries. Seems to know everyone in the family. From the bank, Grandma and I walk to my Uncle Joga-Rao's house. It used to belong to my mother (she had bought it with her share of the inheritance from her father); but the house turned out to be too large for her needs and so Joga-Rao bought it from her.

A pretty, green, two-storey structure; tracery windows with glass shutters. Aunt Rukmini greets me as if she's known me all her life – which she has – but it's as though I went to the corner store and back; as if it hasn't been seven years since we last met, in Boston. Ushers us into the sitting room. There's an elderly man seated on a sofa. Ramumama. Smiles and clasps my hand. "We don't recognize each other," he says, "but we do remember!" It's like seeing your long-lost father, being welcomed like this. Ramumama is retired and widowed; runs a movie theatre and spends the rest of his time solving friends' difficulties. To look at him, you wouldn't guess that he's seventy-two.

Uncle Joga-Rao looks older than he is: smoking has discoloured his teeth; his face is splotchy, the skin sags. After talking for a while we adjourn to the dining room. Have idlis and curry powder – made of crushed green curry leaves, not hot.

Joga-Rao is the only one of my mother's three siblings to stay in India. When I was a boy, he was the only man we knew who owned a car. Sometimes he would take us for drives. The last time I'd seen him, in Boston, he'd been doing research on helicopters for the U.S. Army. My father and I had gone there from Kingston, Ontario, for a long weekend: Canadian Thanksgiving. We were watching the news in their Boston apartment when we learned that the FLQ, the *Front de libération du Québec*, had kidnapped a cabinet minister named Pierre Laporte. It was October 1970.

TAKE A BUS BACK to Grandma's house. Only women are allowed to use the bus's front door, so we enter together through the back door. All the seats are taken, so we stand till someone offers his seat to Grandma. She starts talking to the woman next to her as though they're acquainted. A conductor – wearing something of a brown uniform – sells different coloured tickets according to passengers' destinations. Many of the women have garlands of flowers pinned on their oiled, black hair. The hairstyles of the men are no less fancy than back home; look more artificial here because of the jet blackness of the hair and all that oil. I cling to the overhead bar. Mine is one of the few wrists without a watch.

Where have you been, Babu?
Why, studying in America.

These People: A Politician

MY GRANDFATHER KRISHNA had three children by his first marriage: a girl, a boy and another girl. The eldest two became more successful than their younger sister. On both sides of my vastly extended family, whether people are successful counts for much more than whether they are happy. The youngest child became a teacher; the boy became a singer; the eldest became, of all things, a politician. She was my Aunt Ratna, and her story begins with her marriage, in the 1930s, to a man named Srinivas-Rao, when she changed her name to B. Ratna S. Rao.

My Ratna-Uncle Srinivas was from Chittoor, a South Indian town halfway between Bangalore and Madras. At first, he struggled to establish his law practice and took whatever work he could find. Often his clients paid him with produce instead of money. Since he let them sleep on his verandah while pleading their cases, Aunt Ratna became impatient. She would awake the clients by sweeping the verandah early in the morning. They scurried this way and that, then sat patiently in the compound until Srinivas left the house. Then they followed him to his office. All of this might have continued – he might have become just another barrister –

if it hadn't been for the temple of Lord Venkateswara, our family god on my mother's side.

If Varanasi, once called Benares, is the holiest place in North India, then Tirumala is the holiest place in the South. The temple of Lord Venkateswara stands on the top of a hill that's coiled like a snake. On the seventh coil of the snake. Every South Indian tries to make at least one pilgrimage to the temple during each lifetime. Lord Venkateswara, also called Lord Balaji, is a lesser-known avatar of Lord Vishnu, the Preserver. After incurring a huge debt in heaven to pay for another god's marriage, Vishnu came to earth as Venkateswara so that people could pay off his debt. In return, he would grant any wish made in front of him. A story, perhaps, but one so powerful that the temple containing the image of Venkateswara has collected enough money to repay the debt many times over.

At first pilgrims would throw their offerings – money or, more often, jewellery – into a cauldron as high as a man. For a long time, families who wanted sons would also throw their newborn daughters into the cauldron. If the girls didn't suffocate under the weight of the offerings, they starved. The practice ended sometime in the 19th century. Pilgrims now push their offerings through a slit into a jar. The temple has amassed so much wealth that its pillars are covered with silver and its dome is covered with gold.

By the 1930s or 1940s, the committee running the temple could no longer manage so much wealth. It decided to establish a foundation and hired Srinivas for legal advice. Whenever he and Ratna visited Bangalore when I was a boy, they would stay at my Aunt Mani's house in Jayanagar, on the south side of the city and, in those days, near the outskirts. I looked forward to their visits because they were the only relatives on my father's side who owned a car. It was a Fiat – I remember it as red – and the driver let me play with the horn. If I flicked the switch one way, the horn honked; if I flicked the switch the other way, it beeped. The car also had fog lights, which must have made it a rarity in South India. As one of Ratna's sons later told me, "Fog there, you see, is as common as snow."

My mother and I visited Chittoor once. It might even have been during our pilgrimage to Tirumala. Ratna's house was large and had an inner courtyard. There, one morning, I watched her sons, Murali and Vasu, leave for their secondary school. Both of them had splendid leather bookbags. My father later said that they grew up well because Ratna had trained as a child psychologist. It sounded like an apology for the way he had raised me.

With her husband's career successful, their sons on their way to becoming engineers, and servants to do her bidding, Ratna had status and time. A friend, one of her former classmates, persuaded her to run to become the mayor of Chittoor. She did, she won, and she kept on winning. After a number of years, the friend persuaded her to run for the Rajya Sabha, or Upper House, an elected senate like the one in the U.S. Ratna won again, but she had two advantages: she ran for the Congress Party, which ruled India like a one-party state; and the man who had launched her political career, the friend and former classmate, was the President of India. It was only after I became a civil servant in my mid-twenties that I began wondering whether my grandfather Krishna would have approved of Ratna's vocation. In India, as elsewhere, honesty and politics are incompatible; the word most often associated with politics is pragmatism. Ratna certainly must have been pragmatic, because she continued being re-elected to the Rajya Sabha.

Some months before my first India trip, the Congress Party finally lost a general election because Indira Gandhi had disenchanted voters by declaring Emergency Rule. On the one hand, corruption had nearly faded from the civil service; on the other hand, her eldest son, Sanjay, had been overzealous about sterilizing villagers who knew little about birth control. Indira's declaration had offended the sensibilities of Indian intellectuals, and the Janata Party had capitalized on this disenchantment. In the historic general election of 1977, Ratna displayed her pragmatism by running for the Janata Party. Led by a man named Morarji Desai – ironically best known in the West for his urine-drinking habits – Janata won. Had it been re-elected, Ratna might have become a cabinet minister, but the tenuous collection of dissenters who made up Janata found itself unable to govern for long.

In the winter of 1977-78, the Congress (I) Party – I for Indira or India, it was hard to say which – made a dazzling comeback in state elections. I asked my grandmother why she was voting for the Congress (I) after what had happened during the Emergency. "Indira's father was Jawaharlal Nehru," my grandmother replied. "He helped give us our independence." Ratna could have relented and returned to Indira's fold but she refused. Instead, she quit politics. I would like to think that she didn't relent because her principles wouldn't allow her to switch sides again. More likely, she didn't relent because she had developed cancer – from stress according to my father. That was something Indira Gandhi would never develop, he claimed, because she took relaxing Swiss vacations.

I don't know if Ratna ever abused her position. I hope not. It wasn't the sort of thing I could ask her. I do know that she made full use of her advantages, like the VIP quota. It allowed her to buy appliances and vehicles without having to place her name on waiting lists. This is how, for instance, my cousin Ravi – my Aunt Mani's youngest son – owned the most reliable brand of scooter made in India. If it hadn't been for the quota, he would have had to wait ten years to take delivery.

Before she retired, I took advantage of her position as well. When I left India in the spring of 1978, I had to get a tax clearance saying that my father had supported me during my stay; that I hadn't worked during my five months with him on Debur Road. There were only two ways to certify this. One was to pay a notary for an affidavit. This would cost ten rupees, and I was sure that the notary would give the taxation clerk at least half. My principles wouldn't allow it. The second was to have someone I knew in Delhi come to the office and vouch for me. While I wondered what to do, a young Israeli started crying in the waiting room. Her friends tried comforting her while she sat, bent double, with her long dark hair hiding her face. No one had told her or her friends to keep their foreign exchange receipts to prove that they hadn't worked.

The clerk was unsympathetic.

"You keep cheating us while we travel around your country," she cried, "and now you're trying to cheat us before we can get out? I'm never coming back!"

I could do nothing to help her but I could get my own, small revenge. "I've decided to call someone over to vouch for me," I told the clerk. "Can I use your phone?"

"Whom do you wish to telephone?" he asked.

"My aunt, Mrs. Ratna-Bai. Her office is quite close."

I knew exactly what he would ask: "What is she?" Everyone asks this because in a country as large as India many people have the same name. Besides, it often seems more important what an Indian does than what he or she is called.

I replied innocently, "A Member of the Rajya Sabha."

I've never seen an Indian clerk move so quickly. He dashed through a door and whispered to a man in a cool, dark office:

My mother's people: Joga-Rao, Amba-Rao, Lakshmi and Rama.

an officer. Both of them discussed me while I waited in the doorway. The officer read my form, then signed it while the clerk, sweating from his dash, kept one eye on me.

How could I resist turning the screw? "I could still phone her, you know," I said. "She won't mind coming over."

Even now I wonder what happened to those Israelis; whether I could have or should have done something for them. Whether the one with the long dark hair kept her promise and never went back.

DISTANCES

Wednesday, October 5, 1977

GRANDMA TAKES ME to Joga-Rao's house again, this time leaving me to spend the day. En route we drop some of my shirts with a *dhobi* (a washerman) and shop for a box of sweets for my cousins. Shops face the sidewalk and are open to the street. Smaller shops have a counter to protect the keepers, I suppose, from road and foot traffic; larger shops are set back so you can walk in. Sidewalks are granite slabs set across a ditch at the edge of the road. Some places, the stone's broken and tilts up at an angle. The traffic is mixed: motorized vehicles, bicycles, carts drawn by cattle. Even in a posh middle-class area like this, there are cows for providing milk tethered to many gates.

My youngest cousin – Sinu, short for Srinivas – shows me photos of the family and of Mom and me. The house is named SRINIVAS after him: the youngest, but the only boy. Takes me to see the last house Mom and I lived in before we left India in 1962, when I was six. Turns out it's only two blocks away. A red and white house with blue tracery windows. Through the verandah, I can see two doors. I remember that they led into the main room and into my bedroom. Don't feel nostalgia; just a kind of detached interest.

This is what I remember of that verandah:

I had a tutor in the second standard, what I would learn to call grade two in Canada. He came after school and we sat on the verandah floor while he tutored. Thanks to him, I could add impressive sums – five columns wide, seven rows high – and carry numbers in my head. One day, no matter how quickly I added, I couldn't please him. He pointed at our low wicker table and said that if I didn't try harder he would drop the table on my head. I started crying and he left, disgusted. When my mother came home, Mary told her what had happened. My mother sent Mary to fetch the tutor. Soon I heard shouts from the verandah. I crept from my room to see my mother scolding him. He sat cross-legged on the floor with his back against the wall and his hands clasped. He kept bobbing over his hands, begging her forgiveness, and I watched her reduce him to silence. I felt no triumph; only awe. Finally she said, "Get out." He did, and he never came back. She gave Mary a rupee and she took me for a walk. She let me hold the rupee while we shopped, and I bought a tin of biscuits.

Why should I remember this, of all things, when so much more happened in that verandah? It was where I used to play while waiting for my mother to come home from the Institute, the Indian Institute of Science, where my father and my uncles had also studied. It was where we used to entertain my grandfather, Krishna, when he visited. It was where my mother sat to read and write aerograms to England and Canada and America. I think the first letter I ever read – I know the first letter that I ever wrote – was an aerogram. It was the one in which I asked my father whether he would be meeting us at the airport in Canada with a Chevrolet.

I sit in my aunt and uncle's living room after lunch. Joga-Rao comes home for it. Am sleepy but join in a joke session with the youngest four children. My cousins:

Lakshmi – short for Venkatlakshmi, my maternal grand-mother's name – is the eldest, one month younger than me. Quite brilliant and studies a lot. She takes after Mom this way. People call her Bujji.

Shakuntala – called Chinni, which means smaller or younger –is the second one. She's pretty and more lively; was my favourite when I lived here. She's also brilliant.

The other three were born after I left; only met them once before, also in Boston, back in October of 1970:

Saraswati – called Rani, is next. She's noisier and more outgoing than her sisters. Mom would consider Rani's great-est liability her somewhat darker skin.

Padmavati – called Paddy, is the fourth. She looks a bit like Chinni. Very quiet but has a way of breaking in with insight-ful and amusing remarks.

Sinu's the fifth and was unplanned, as Mom told me once. He's thirteen at most; outspoken, humorous, and holds his own against the four girls.

Their parents, my uncle and aunt:

Joga-Rao's an aeronautical engineer and no less brilliant than Mom or her twin sister, my Aunt Rama, who married an astronomer from Kerala. Joga-Rao often visits the States and likes to boast about his duties and privileges at the Insti-tute. He smokes a pipe. Like the others, Joga-Rao has to worry about the level of his blood sugar.

Rukmini's the perfect wife and mother. Tells me she con-siders her sole duty that of running their house and how proud she is of this. Is helped in the kitchen by one part-time servant; another woman sweeps the floors.

For the rest of the afternoon, Sinu and I play French cricket. He likes making me run after the ball. In the front and back yards are coconut palms; also jackfruit, grapefruit, sandalwood and gooseberry trees. And there's a scraggly pine: my Christmas tree when I was five. In a back room, among Mom's things, we find a pink jumpsuit, one she embroidered for me with a steam engine. Also find my grandfather's pocket watch, a Zenith about fifty years old. Guess it's supposed to be mine someday. Doesn't work.

⇥⁕⇤

AFTER RUKMINI'S NAP, she takes me to see Lady Raman, the widow of Sir C.V. Raman, who won the Nobel Prize for chemistry nearly fifty years ago. Lady Raman acted as Mom's guardian – a godmother of sorts – when we lived here. Her house is nearby, and I'm surprised at the short distances between the important places of my childhood. Seems like the distances were a lot greater then. One day Sinu will notice this as well. For now he looks up to me like the elder brother he never had.

The house is huge and many sided; two storeys; a large, two-level sitting room. Under the front portico: an Ambassador automobile with old-style signalling flags in the door pillars. They pop out to signal a turn. There's at least one manservant and two women. The yard in front of the house is so large that it could be a park. It's protected by a wall topped with barbed wire. In the sitting room are photos of Lady Raman's parents, paintings of her and Lord Raman, reproductions of classical drawings of bejewelled women. In the cabinets are two ivory carvings of the Taj Mahal and other souvenirs. On one shelf are three violin cases; in the far half of the sitting room is a disused piano. I try it. Most of its keys are inaudible, others barely work.

Lady Raman is over eighty. Sits in a wooden chair and wears a white sari-like dress with a heavy shawl. Kerchief tied on her head. Her face is brown and shrunken but not as wrinkled as I'd expected. Grey hairs grow on her upper lip and chin; give her a visible moustache and even whiskers. She wears glasses. She speaks faintly and recognizes my name only when Rukmini mentions Mom. Lady Raman has forgotten Joga-Rao's name. She addresses me but we speak little. She and Rukmini chat for nearly half an hour while Sinu and I look around. At one point Lady Raman says, "The world turns once a day but the mind turns a thousand times." Referring to someone's indecisiveness.

When they discuss my mother, Lady Raman recalls the way Mom chafed at being confined to bed after I was born – she was so eager to return to work. "She should never have gotten married," Lady Raman says. "One must make a decision whether to look after the house or a career."

—≫≪—

SINU TAKES ME to see Cluny Convent, where I attended nursery school and my first two standards. The layout's just as I remembered but the distances and dimensions have changed. The hill between the front offices and the school is a low rise climbed by two dozen steps, if that. The large compound behind, where we played and, after lunch, said the Lord's Prayer in the sunlight, is just a schoolyard. The distance from the girls' wing to the children's school is negligible. There are also things I don't remember: a painted statue of Saint Joseph set high in a niche; miniature chairs and tables in what must have been my classroom. Sinu takes me back past the park where I played. It's near Ramumama's house.

After high tea including *idlis*, my favourite snack, Joga-Rao gives me a thousand rupees (then about $250). Mom asked him to do this. Then he drives me back to Grandma's house. It's the first time he's been to the new house. He doesn't come in; only calls greetings to her from the car. I think it's the same, small brown car that he drove when I was a boy.

—⚹—

Why such detachment, so little nostalgia?
It's like being trapped in an aerogram. Not as though someone else is writing this.
Someone else is. Whomever kept the journals, at any rate. Someone young who thought he had to sound older than he was.
As I was saying, it's as though someone wrote an aerogram about my childhood and posted it. And it got lost forever.
It being the aerogram? Or your childhood?

Babu (Ven) on my first birthday in Benares (now Varanasi) in March of 1957; I am holding a red car, a gift from my Uncle Amba-Rao.

THESE PEOPLE: A SINGER

MY GRANDFATHER KRISHNA named his eldest son Chaitanya after
a Hindu saint. The original Chaitanya had been a teacher
during the 16th century in Bengal. After a vivid trance, he
became a devotee of Lord Vishnu the Preserver and spread
Vaishnavism throughout India. Chaitanya followed the
bhakti, or devotional, tradition and chanted the Lord's name
loud and long with his fine voice. My Uncle Chaitanya may
not have been a religious man but he, too, had a fine voice.

Sometime during the 1930s Krishna returned to his ances-
tral village of Nelawanki and tried to persuade the villagers
to move southwest. To encourage resettlement, Mysore State
was waiving water and other taxes for five years to anyone
willing to farm the rich soil of the Kabini Valley. But the villagers of Nelawanki told Krishna that God must have put
them here for some reason and they refused to move.

Perhaps because of this, Krishna decided that Chaitanya
should study agriculture. But he wanted to study music. Frus-
trated with college, he left South India for the north. Here he
landed a job as a playback singer for a film studio. Playback
singers perform the songs that are apparently sung on screen
by actors. He had firm ideas about how the songs should be

sung, and these conflicted with the ideas of music directors. Whether Chaitanya quit or whether he was fired doesn't matter. He returned to college to study music and earned his doctorate. Altogether, he studied at the universities of Madras, Benares and Poona. And then, in the early 1940s, he became involved in Mahatma Gandhi's Quit India movement.

By now, Gandhi had become a formidable force. He declared that the British presence in India was only serving to provoke the Japanese, who had invaded Burma in early 1942 and were poised to invade India. No one doubted that the British would leave; the question was when and under what conditions. When turned out to be August of 1947; the major condition turned out to be partitioning the subcontinent into Hindu India and Muslim Pakistan. The real political power was already being claimed by Indian aristocrats, men like Jawaharlal Nehru. Still, Gandhi ensured that his Quit India movement remained populist. It especially appealed to students like Chaitanya – fiery young men who gladly defied orders like those that prohibited political demonstrations. One day he found himself in one; family legend even claims that he led it. Swinging their *lathis*, bamboo poles weighted with lead, mounted policemen charged. Chaitanya fell under a horse and broke his wrist.

My father, who was studying in Bangalore, was also involved in the Quit India movement, but his involvement went no further than organizing speeches. This was why he was surprised one day to receive a visit from two members of the CID, the Criminal Investigation Department. Chaitanya had gone into hiding and the CID suspected he might try to contact my father. I don't know whether this actually happened, but the two brothers had remained close even though Chaitanya had broken with the rest of the family. After the war and Independence, he remained in the north to finish his studies while his wife raised their family. He left India rarely, most notably to be a research associate for a year at Cologne University in what was then West Germany. He later visited the University of Moscow. He listed his specialties as the psychophysics of Indian music, ethnomusicology, and the study of musical instruments.

I stayed with him in New Delhi on my way back to Canada in March, 1978. He was taller than me and robust, like my father; yet I remember Chaitanya huddled in a chair. He tried to stay warm with a shawl around his shoulders and an orange beret from his European days on his balding head. It was cool in Delhi even in March. He was in his mid-to-late fifties by now, assistant secretary for music at the Sangeet Natak Akademi, the National Arts Academy. He published under the name B.C. Deva, an abbreviation of Begamudré Chaitanya-Deva. In a shop on the thoroughfare near his house I found his latest book in English, *Musical Instruments*.

The house was one of over a hundred row houses crammed back to back into one block; they looked identical, as though built from the same batch of grey concrete. His house was large enough for half a dozen people: Chaitanya and his wife, Sindhu; their college-aged children, a boy nicknamed Bundu and a girl nicknamed Babli; and Sindhu's widowed mother. Chaitanya's eldest children were both girls, one nicknamed Dilli, the other Kukki. They lived with their husbands but Dilli had come home to have her first child. There's a saying in India: "Come home soon." According to Hindu tradition, a first child should be born in the house of the wife's parents, and everyone hopes that she will come home soon – to deliver a son.

In the evenings, after I had seen the big shopping area called Connaught Place or taken the Agra Express to see the Taj Mahal and Agra Fort – where Shah Jahan's son imprisoned him so that he wouldn't bankrupt the treasury by building a mausoleum for himself that was identical to the Taj Mahal but in black marble – my Uncle Chaitanya and I sat in his study. It was also the living room of the house, but the women used the large kitchen as their living room. The few times he referred to our family, he called them "these people." Sometimes, to make a point, he rubbed his wrist, which ached from the cold and damp. "These people," he said, "have their fancy cars and their hundred acres of rice lands. What do they know of the real India?" He meant not his elder sister, my Aunt Mani, but his younger sister, my Aunt Ratna, who had married so well and, in his view, was too full of herself. She also lived in Delhi for much of the year but she and Chaitanya rarely met.

We spent a week of evenings like this in the study/living room. Whenever his eyebrows began to knit like barbed wire, whenever his eyes nearly vanished because he was squinting at the world – trying to make sense of it – I steered him back to music or art or our saintly ancestor, Raghavendra Swami. Once I even showed Chaitanya the prologue to my ambitious novel, "Nomads." He suggested, and not in a very kindly way, that Raghavendra's powers of healing were incidental to his intellectual and spiritual powers. Chaitanya seemed incapable of showing kindness except to his grandchildren, but that was different. They weren't old enough yet to betray him.

Because of his manner, I never told him that even more than a writer I longed to be a musician. As a boy, I had studied piano for two years and violin for a year, but learned to play neither. No wonder it surprised him when, one morning, I asked if I could accompany him to work. I spent the entire morning at the National Arts Academy. He proudly showed me the music library next to his office. He called it "my

library." Shelf after shelf contained reel-to-reel tapes that doc-
umented folk music: the contemporary music of rural India
handed down through generations but never written down.
That evening he said nothing about my visit but he seemed
more relaxed, grateful that someone in our extended family
– one of "these people" – appreciated him at last.

A few years later, after he retired, Chaitanya moved back
to Bangalore. Here he died of a heart attack. He died neither
quickly nor quietly. He spent his last hours bellowing at the
doctors and nurses with his once fine voice. He screamed at
the pains in his chest. He spent his last hours cursing all
those people who, as far as he knew, had never cared enough
about India or about music and, despite all that he had done,
never would.

This is not how I like to remember him, though. I often
take his book *Musical Instruments* down from my shelf and
read passages at random. A passage like this one:

> Perhaps the reader has heard the music of the Nagas of the
> eastern provinces of India or of the Todas of hills [the Nil-
> giri Hills] in Tamil Nadu. These people have a kind of
> shuffling movement — their dance — accompanied by howls
> and screeches, resembling their hunting calls. The whole
> performance has a strange feeling of rhythm and melody.
> And, if you compare these 'sounds' with the high intricacy
> of raga and tale, they may not sound 'musical'. Yet there is
> much 'music' there and many a raga and tale has, who
> knows, its first fountains in these non-musical acts of
> howling.

Or a passage like this one, in which my Uncle Chaitanya's
voice and his proud, scholarly manner still sing:

What is true of music in general is more evident with in-struments. Many scholars — and, of course, there are many who dispute the point — are of the opinion that quite pos-sibly the idea of making a harp originated in the twang of the hunting or martial bow and the plectrum in the arrow. Indeed, when Ravana enters the final battle against Rama [in the Hindu epic *Ramayanna*], he proudly says, "Rama does not know of my skill in war. I shall play the veena of my bow with the plectrum of my arrow; and the hearts of my enemies will tremble and they will flee in disarray."

My father, Rakosh, at the National Research Council in Ottawa in the early 1960s.

Shirts, Sandals, Sanskrit

Thursday, October 6, 1977

MAKE THREE OR FOUR TRIPS to the mailbox. Answer a letter from David S.; also write to John H. and Mom – then still in Canada and teaching at York University – describing the last few days. Not everything, though. She worries too much. In the evening, Grandma and I go shopping near the Bangalore Corporation Building. Mom brought me here to get my vaccinations before we left India. The streets are packed. Bangalore's no different from any large western city. Westerners want to come to the east to find peace when all they need to do is escape into the countryside – the way I did during most of those five weeks in Britain before flying here.

The shirts we look at are too bright. I buy one knitted shirt in a shopping centre. That's what they call it here when two or more stores are joined. Across the road, in Handloom House, I buy three Indian-style shirts with tunic collars and loose tails that can't be tucked into trousers. The ceiling of the shop is wood, recessed in places. On some of the squares are star designs in different colours of wood. Really nice. After this, we buy a pair of sandals for me to wear instead of shoes. I'm going to end up looking like a western-educated Indian. Which is what I am anyways.

Light supper of *masala dosa* and *gulab jamun* in an air conditioned restaurant. Grandma leaves a twenty-five *paise* tip for a bill of six rupees. Behind her back I add another twenty-five *paise*. Again she argues with the autorickshaw driver because he wants to take a longer route. All over a few *paise*. When we reach home, she tells me the clothes and sandals, instead of being paid for from the thousand rupees given to me by my Uncle Joga-Rao, are a gift from her.

Friday, October 7, 1977

IN THE EVENING we go to CT's house, following the directions she gave over the phone. CT is short for Chinnathally, a distant cousin of my mother's. First we take a bus, which takes half an hour to arrive, then an autorickshaw. CT and I are happy to see one another. She hasn't changed since I saw her in Toronto two or three years ago. Her house is a huge, two-storey affair. She keeps a staff of three: two girls from her village and an aged driver. Her mother's also here. CT's mother is famous in the family: the wife of Sir Sonti Ramamurthy, once acting governor of either Bombay or Madras, not sure which. But he was the first Indian to hold this position. Like Lady Raman, CT's mother is in her eighties. Understands most of what we say in English but is quiet. She has trouble sitting for long, or standing, or even walking very far. CT gives us *wada* to eat. Am getting leery of fried foods; they're upsetting my stomach. Also gives us sweets; these, I like: I've inherited the Sunti sweet tooth, Mom said once.

Grandma and CT haven't met since my parents' wedding, over twenty years ago. My return seems to be bringing people together.

Later, we go by CT's car to the Bharathiya Vidhya Bhavan, the Indian Cultural Centre, where CT attends Upanishad classes. I stay less than half an hour. The class starts late because of rain. The teacher's a man in his sixties with a bald head and a face like a coconut with a jaw. Speaks as though his mouth is full of marbles. There's a long, red, vertical stripe on his brow. His name is Anantharanachar, of the Iyengar caste (a Brahmin of Tamil origin); has a PhD in Sanskrit. There's an old man who monopolizes conversation and has a comment for every one of the teacher's. Another old man wears a long, black coat. The three horizontal lines on his brow stand for – loosely translated – physical, mental, and moral qualities; he's a follower of Lord Shiva. The class follows the teacher in a prayer chant. Then he reads today's passage, in Sanskrit. He doesn't so much say the lines; he sings them. Keeps repeating the English translation and changes a word each time. The verse: "Oh Lord, remove the brightness from your face so that I may behold the most auspicious form of yourself."

Why does this sound familiar?

Because of Lord Venkateswara at Tirumala, our family god. It's not that his face is bright, though. He keeps his eyes covered so that he won't see all the evil in the world – see all of the parents who would throw their baby girls into the offering pot – and then, with a blinding flash, destroy this world of ours.

But then he can't see the good, either.

This is true.

These People: A Teacher

My grandfather Krishna's second daughter was Navamani, known as Mani. Her story also begins with her marriage – as did her sister's – to a man named Srinivas. A handsome man. Like Ratna, Mani did not mean to have a career. It was forced on her by a familiar twist of fate: she found herself with four children to raise alone.

Unlike my grandfather Krishna, my Mani-Uncle Srinivas was an ambitious man; also unlike my grandfather, Srinivas was not a lucky man. That is to say, he lacked the talent and discipline that, in turn, attract luck. He became the manager of a textile mill in Mysore City and bought a large house. Mani entertained often; and, according to my father, she bought a new sari every day. Even if it was only one sari a week, she and Srinivas did live beyond their means. Worse, he assumed that the mill would run itself. He sank into debt, fled India, and settled in England. Here, he lived with a classical Indian dancer. Mani found herself trying to raise four children even as Srinivas's creditors tried to collect his debts. The creditors sent *goondas*, hired thugs, to intimidate her. They even threatened to harm the children. The family lived in fear. Once, when my father knocked at the door of the house, the children ran screaming into the back.

A twist of fate saved Mani. She had an admirer, a former classmate. One day he came to the house and confessed his love for her. He placed a stack of rupees on the kitchen table, told her to pay off the debts, and left the house. It was all he could do. He could never hope to marry her because she was already married. Besides, he was not Hindu; he was Muslim.

By now, Krishna had remarried and had fathered two more sons, my father and his younger brother, Ananda. This youngest boy proved rebellious even at an early age; he hated school and kept running away. Mani decided to become his teacher. Before long, other parents brought her their difficult children, and she found herself with what eventually became a certified school. After Krishna retired and built himself a house in Bangalore, in the outlying district called Jayanagar, he built Mani a house in the same district. This second house was close enough that he could visit but far enough that he could remain aloof. "I have helped all of you through your troubles," he said. "Now leave me in peace." Attached to Mani's new house was a large room which she used as her school.

When I was a child, my mother took me to Mani's house often. I played with my cousins, two girls named Gita and Radha and two boys named Krishna and Ravi. Once, I remember, they were making an elaborate game from empty cigarette packets on the schoolroom floor. The game was to stand the packets on end, tip one over, and see how many of the others also tipped. Another time, I saw a new electric train on the floor. Ravi, who was older than me but closest in age, claimed that their father had sent it. It didn't seem strange that my cousins' father lived in another country; so did my own father, who was studying in America. When I asked my mother about the train, she said, "Your Mani-Uncle Srinivas has returned to India from England. He visits your cousins secretly because he does not want to be arrested by the police." She didn't tell me why he should be arrested and I didn't believe he was back because I never saw him. Later, I wondered whether my grandfather had, himself, bought the train.

Better than the cigarette-packet game and electric train, I remember the pictures. They were coloured pictures of animals on the schoolroom walls. Once, when I was five, Ravi took me by the hand and led me to one of them. "Can you read this?" he asked. "What does it say?" And I, proud of how much I was learning in school, read aloud, "I am a...pig." Ravi shrieked with laughter and clutched his sides. "Babu is a pig!" he cried. "Babu is a –!"

Years later, when I returned for my first India trip, Ravi came to my grandmother's pink house and took me to Jayanagar. When Radha entered the room, I thought she was my Aunt Mani because Radha looked so much like the Mani I'd known as a boy. Then Mani herself entered. She looked old; her puffed face was splotchy. She would have been in her sixties. I didn't know it, but she was ill. Among other things, she was suffering from diabetes. Our reunion was a pleasant one. She brought me a plate of *bondas*, round fritters similar to *wadas*. "I made some especially for you," she said. "You do not eat hot food any more, do you?" I said no – I didn't because I'd grown up Canadian – and took three. While I bit into the first *bonda*, it never occurred to me to wonder why Ravi was watching me so closely. Everyone I met watched me closely – sometimes, I thought, to make sure there was still a family resemblance, because I sounded so foreign, with my Canadian accent. When I bit into the second *bonda*, my mouth burned. This time Ravi didn't shriek and clutch his sides. He laughed like a man while Mani and Radha scolded him for playing yet another practical joke on me.

Ravi was still unmarried but Radha was married to an engineer named Jagadish. They lived in the district of Bangalore called Malleswaram, where I'd lived as a boy with my mother. Radha and Jagadish had two children, a girl and a boy. I spent much time at both houses: Mani's in Jayanagar, Radha's in Malleswaram. My eldest cousins, Gita and Krishna, were also married but lived elsewhere, she in Hyderabad, he in Bangalore's Brahmin Quarter. And now I finally met my Mani-Uncle Srinivas. He no longer paid clandestine visits; he lived in Bangalore. He had become a devotee of a famous guru and lived in a room attached to the guru's Bangalore office in a posh district called Palace Orchards. My father claimed that Srinivas had returned only to claim Mani's estate after she died. I said nothing. I had no use for family jealousies. It was enough that I was fulfilling a promise to myself: to see as many of my relatives as I could.

I spent one of my most enjoyable afternoons of that trip at Radha and Jagadish's house. We gathered there for a holiday. It was my turn to play a joke on Ravi. I told him I would bring some sugar cane, and I did: an entire stalk of sugar cane six feet long, leaves and all. How we laughed. Mani was there; so was Srinivas. So were other relatives, a dozen in all. I sat and listened while they spoke in a mixture of Kannada and English, often in the same sentence, and found myself able to follow almost everything. My cousins had grown up, Mani had grown old, but in some ways it felt as though nothing had changed. The comfort of it: to have a real family, and close at hand.

It was early January 1978, the last time I would see Mani alive.

TWO OF THESE PEOPLE

Saturday, October 8, 1977

I AWAKEN EARLY and set out for Bangalore Railway Station to buy my ticket for tomorrow. Not even nine o'clock and it's already hot. Old and not so old men sit around picking at their feet; children – some naked below the waist – wander around or take a shit; fruit sellers lie behind their baskets as though not expecting to sell a thing. Once, I take a woman aback by asking her which way the railway station is. Guess it's not done here to talk to strange women. The station's newer and cleaner than Bombay's Victoria Terminus. I wait in line barely fifteen minutes.

Back to Grandma's house. She takes me to the nearby Gandhi Bhavan. We watch the end of a drama while waiting for the museum to be unlocked. The area's a clearing topped by a thatched, sloping roof with a stage at one end; this is bounded on two sides by a concrete building. People, mostly women, sit on carpets that cover this clearing. We watch from a second-storey balcony. On stage, a woman laments the death of her husband, who lies on a bier. After the curtain comes down, the actors rise to sing. When the curtain rises again, orange-robed musicians play to one side of the stage while an actress waves a lamp in front of a life-sized statue of Lord Krishna. He holds a wooden flute. The statue is surrounded by garlands of fresh flowers like marigolds.

Then the statue moves: it's not a statue, after all; it's a performer.

The Gandhi Picture Gallery contains photos of Mahatma Gandhi arranged chronologically. Even after pictures of his funeral, there are photos of him to symbolize the immortality of his work. Also two full-sized portraits, a bust, and a collection of letters to different people including Leo Tolstoy and Annie Besant. Good copies.

AT FOUR O'CLOCK my Aunt Mani's youngest son, Ravi, comes to fetch me. He's about 25 now. Has an engineering degree but works as an electrician in a factory. It's closed, thanks to a strike. With him is a girl of seven or so, one of his nieces: Janaki. We take an autorickshaw past Handloom House to Jayanagar District. It's more built up than I remembered. Inside the house is a woman too young to be Mani. It's Radha, one of Ravi's two older sisters. With her is her son, Haymanth, Janaki's younger brother, who's three or four. Looks like my father in an early photo: plump, with a round face but with a snub nose. In a doorway hangs a sheet instead of a door. Mani enters through this doorway from another room. She looks old and she is – sixty-three or so – and her face is more splotchy than wrinkled. The first half hour is difficult. Large gaps in the conversation. Ravi sits silently in a corner and lets Mani and Radha do the work. Everyone relaxes once the food arrives. There's *wada*, again, and a sweet made from cream of wheat and milk with raisins and nuts. Haymanth is still shy but coming closer to me. Radha brings me more *wadas*. The last one is hot. She looks as surprised as I do when I have to gulp some water. Mani's also surprised. She'd expected that

I wouldn't like my food too hot and was careful to keep the ordinary *wadas* separate from the mild ones. Ravi starts laughing. Fifteen years, and he still plays practical jokes. Still, this breaks the ice.

Radha takes me to a temple across the street. It's dedicated to the god-king Rama, whose wife Sita (also known as Janaki) was kidnapped by the evil King of Lanka. We leave our sandals outside. Inside is a large hall. At one end is the shrine, served by a priest wearing a dhoti, and across his shoulder is the sacred Brahmin thread. We walk clockwise around the shrine and stop in front of it. The priest rings a bell for Rama's attention while passing a lamp in a high, clockwise circle. Then he takes a dented, tin plate out of a niche that contains statues of a god and goddess, both gaily painted. On the plate is a lamp. We put coins on this plate. Then the priest gives us sacred water, which we hold in cupped hands and drink. He holds a bell-like metal cap over our heads, then gives us each a flower. Radha prostrates herself on the stone floor for a few seconds. Later we sit and watch, Radha and I with Janaki. A father holds his son high so that he can reach and ring the bell. Maybe it's not to attract the god's attention, though; maybe it's to drive away evil spirits. Wish I knew more. This used to be my home, after all.

RAVI TAKES ME to the railway station to see our Aunt Ratna, the senator. He drives a new scooter, a model known for its reliability. They have to be ordered ten years in advance, but he waited only six months for his because he got it under Ratna's parliamentary quota. He's only driven a moped before the scooter, and I have no helmet, but we set off. At first I'm nervous but I force myself to laugh. Soon enjoy the ride; feel sorry for people on foot and in buses.

Ratna's been put up in one of the station retiring rooms. The others are also occupied by MPs or senators who have come to Bangalore for a railway committee meeting. There are about a dozen boys in the corridor to serve the six rooms. Room number one is actually three: an outer sitting room, a bedroom with two beds and a sitting area, and a western-style bathroom. We're attended by a uniformed servant in blue pyjamas and a cap. Again, gaps in the conversation. Ratna's in her late fifties, I think. Except for her white hair, she looks younger. Wears blue-tinted glasses that match her sari and blouse. We talk about my wanting to become a writer – everyone expects me to become a civil servant – and about the Indian railways. The servant brings some dry *chappatis*. While tasting the *sambar*, I eat a hot chilli, which amuses Ravi again.

Ratna says the end of January, Republic Day, is a good time to be in Delhi. Maybe I can combine this with my trip to Rangoon? According to her, if I want to meet "B.B.", our relative who walked back to India from northern Burma, I'll have to go all the way to Rajasthan, in northwestern India. Ravi drops me at Grandma's house and I promise that I'll call when I'm back in Bangalore.

Before leaving, he says firmly that he doesn't think it's a good idea for me to go looking for our Burmese relatives like this. Says some people claim they're all mad.

—※※—

Why this fixation on Burma?

Because, if my grandfather Krishna's elder brothers hadn't run away to Burma, my great-grandfather wouldn't have lost his land and we wouldn't have become city folk. Because, if my great-grandmother hadn't insisted that Krishna finish school, we wouldn't have become educated and ended up as we did in North America.

And if you hadn't ended up there, you wouldn't be such a stranger now?

It's not that I feel like a stranger. A lot of this seems familiar to me. I've come back, but I want to go back farther. I want to research and write that novel, "Nomads."

You won't, though.

How do you know?

Trust me. You'll spend many, many years avoiding writing that novel. But that's all right. You're writing this now, aren't you? Remember what they say – the people who know about such things: "Don't write because you have to tell a story; write because you have a story to tell."

Indian Institute of Science science girls in March of 1953; Rama and Lakshmi are seated at the left.

91

THE MEANING OF ANANDA

Rakosh, and his younger brother, Ananda, in Bangalore in 1928.

1

ANANDA MEANS HAPPINESS or joy. It's another name for Shiva the Destroyer, who must destroy the universe so that it can be recreated. It's also another name for Bala-Rama, the elder brother of Lord Krishna, the eighth avatar of Vishnu the Preserver. But the Ananda we know best was Buddha's foremost disciple.

Buddha's enemies tried to have him killed three times: once by corrupting a prince whose father was Buddha's patron; a second time by rolling a boulder down a hillside; and a third time by inciting an elephant to crush him. Ananda remained steadfast. He could not be corrupted. He watched the boulder split in two even as it rolled downhill. And when others fled the elephant's path, Ananda stayed while Buddha calmly approached it. Overcome by his spiritual power, the elephant fell to its knees and touched its head to the earth.

It was to Ananda that Buddha made what's called one of the most famous speeches in religious history:

> Therefore, O Ananda, be ye islands unto yourselves. Take the Self as your refuge. Take yourself to no external refuge. Hold fast to the Dhamma as an island. Hold fast as a refuge to the truth. Look not for refuge to anyone besides yourselves... And whosoever, Ananda, shall take the Self as an island, taking themselves to no external refuge, but holding fast to Truth as their refuge, it is they, Ananda, who shall reach the very topmost height — but they must be anxious to learn.

Later, when Buddha announced the time had arrived for him to die, Ananda prepared Buddha's bed in a grove of trees that were flowering out of season.

Whether it means happiness or joy, Ananda is a feature of self-realization. Ananda also means bliss.

2

FIRST, I REMEMBER the cage.

A four-year-old in a chair too big for him waits in the lobby of a Bombay hotel. He might be only three. He and his mother have just arrived from Nairobi and, before that, from

Mauritius. They aren't staying at the hotel; they're staying at a Bombay Auntie's house. The mother fans herself with an illustrated magazine. Elsewhere in the lobby, a man perched on a high stool appears to doze. Something metallic shrieks.

Black cables lower a cage to the lobby. The man rises to slide a wooden door out of sight. In the cage, a crisscross of black bars, stands a woman holding a baby. The man scissors the bars out of sight, as well. Ignoring him, she steps out. The boy's mother rises and the boy struggles out of his chair to follow her across the lobby.

The boy's mother tells the woman his name and touches his head. She touches him often, and he likes this. He stares silently at the woman because she is different. She lives in a hotel, and she doesn't fuss over him like other aunties. They all say he has his mother's nose or his father's smile. Such things mean nothing to the boy.

The mother leads the woman into a dining room while asking her questions. The boy lags behind. He wants to see the black bars scissor out of their hiding place, but he's frightened of the man. When the boy and his mother stopped on their way back to India, a girl in Nairobi Auntie's house would lock him in a closet for fun. Although its doors had been louvered, he doesn't like places that are small and dim. He runs for the dining room now. He wants to see the baby.

Next, I remember the stories.

There was once a boy named Ananda, often called Anand. He was born in India late in 1927. He hated nursery school and kept running away until his eldest sister, much older than him, started a school in her house. Nearly everyone in the family wore glasses. He didn't need glasses but he wanted them, so his father bought him a pair with clear lenses. Anand soon lost the lenses, one by one, and then the frame itself. He often got what he wanted and then lost it.

His brother, Rakosh, was older by a year and a half. When Rakosh suddenly left for boarding school, Anand wanted to go, as well. Again he got his way. He seemed to like this school and yet, when the time came for him to follow Rakosh into secondary school, Anand refused. He wanted to go to sea. The boys' father was dumbfounded. No one in the family had gone to sea. The boys' mother was upset, but she could deny Anand nothing, for he was her favourite son. And so he joined the merchant marine as a cadet. Instead of graduating from college shortly after Rakosh did, Anand received his commission in the merchant marine. He became a ship's engineer. Not a first engineer, but even he couldn't expect to start that high.

In 1951, Rakosh went to Japan to work and study. This suited Anand, whose ship often docked in Yokohama. That the Korean War had begun has little bearing on this story except that Japan was still under American occupation. It was a strange place then. Sometimes, in the shops, customers stared in fascination while owners showed off the scorched skin on their arms or necks. These owners had lived in Hiroshima or Nagasaki at the end of the last war and had survived the atomic bomb with little more than skin that was oddly scorched. Japan was also a good place to be Indian. During the recent war crimes trials, an Indian judge had said that Imperial Japanese officers had simply followed orders during the Second World War. The officers had still been hanged, but this Indian judge had became a hero to the Japanese. Rakosh left in 1953, even as the Korean War, by coincidence, ended. By now both he and Anand were engaged. Their fiancées were Japanese.

As it turned out, Rakosh's fiancée released him from their engagement because he wanted to marry someone else. She was Indian like him. They met shortly after he returned to

India. Anand, however, married his Japanese fiancée. She was older than him and this surprised no one except, perhaps, his mother. He and his wife had great expectations for their future. His steamship company headquartered in Bombay and, while he worked at sea, Anand paid for a new flat on Malabar Hill. His mother helped. He hoped to settle in the flat but he never did. Soon he was posted to London, to manage the company's office there. His Japanese wife struggled to learn English. She lost her first child, then gave birth to a second child who lived. She gave him a Japanese name: Shinobu.

One day Anand's superior absconded to South America with the office bank account. So the story goes. When the company ordered Anand back to Bombay while it decided where to post him next, he said he would return only if he was made chief engineer. The company refused, so he quit. The company retaliated by freezing his assets. Why, it's not clear; perhaps it felt he'd been partly to blame for his superior's crime. Anand wouldn't be able to use his flat on Malabar Hill; he couldn't even return to India. His wife went back to Japan with Shinobu, who would have had an elder brother had that boy not been stillborn. On her way back to Japan, she stopped in Bombay and stayed in a hotel. She hadn't been declared persona non grata like her husband. And Anand? He disappeared.

In 1963 or '64, the boy who disliked small, dim places was living in Canada. His parents discussed Anand and his family without realizing the boy, now seven or eight, remembered much of what they said. Even if he didn't understand something, he remembered it. One day in winter the phone rang, and a man asked to speak to the boy's father. Rakosh was in the bathroom and the boy said so. The man still wanted to speak to him, and so the boy knocked on the bathroom door. His father came out scowling. The boy went to his room and closed the door in case he'd done something wrong. The next thing he heard was his father's shout: "Ananda? Where have you been!"

Anand was calling from a hotel on New York's waterfront. He asked whether Rakosh would adopt Shinobu because Anand's wife was finding it difficult to raise their son alone on what little money Anand could send her now. He was taking whatever work he could find on whatever ship would have him – certainly not as a first engineer or even a second. Rakosh said of course. Anand had known that Rakosh would say this. Once, in Japan, Rakosh had given everything he owned to victims of a flood. He was that kind of man. As it turned out, Shinobu never came to Canada. A church group intervened to say that he shouldn't be separated from his parents, and so his mother managed as best she could.

The boy heard all of this a year and a half after the phone call. It was now summer, and he was returning by car from a historic site called Upper Canada Village. The boy was disappointed. He would have liked having a brother. It would have made up for not having a mother because she worked in a different city than his father. And because maybe, just maybe, his father wouldn't keep scowling at him for every little thing. The boy was getting tired of hiding.

Finally, I remember the stamps and the gifts.

A teenager who collects postage stamps receives packets of them from Geneva. This is where his Uncle Anand, his aunt whose name no one seems to remember, and his cousin Shinobu, this is where they all now live. Sometimes the packets come from Japan, from places like Osaka during the World's Fair. Other times, two or three stamps come on the back of a postcard. These are from places like Singapore and, once, on the back of a 3D picture of a radio tower. In Moscow. The stamps from Japan are understandable, but what's Uncle Anand doing in Singapore and Moscow? Is he a spy?

The aunt sends Lindt chocolates. They're like no chocolates the teenaged boy has seen: flat squares that melt all too quickly on the tongue. The boxes are coloured silver or gold. The hard cellophane compartments holding the chocolates don't stay full for long. Nor do they stay empty for long. The boy uses them to store his duplicate stamps. Once, the aunt even sends a box of sugared chestnuts. Imagine living in a place where the locals eat sugared chestnuts. One day, the boy promises himself, he will visit there.

Only one thing could be better than such gifts: to meet Anand, because the boy also wants to go to sea. His hero, one of many, is Horatio Hornblower, from the novels by C. S. Forester. The movie *Captain Horatio Hornblower* stars Gregory Peck. Who could be more heroic than the young midshipman who, despite his lowly birth, becomes a lieutenant commanding ships called *Hotspur* and *Atropos*? Who could be more heroic than the skilled and lucky captain who falls in love with the Duke of Wellington's sister in *The Happy Return*? Who is later knighted by the king and becomes a commodore and then an admiral and finally a lord? Who indeed?

3

I FINALLY MET Uncle Ananda in the summer of 1975. I'd always wanted to see Paris but felt I had to justify it by studying, and so I'd enrolled at the Paris campus of a college that attracted mainly Americans. There, I hoped the French course would finally make me a good Canadian: bilingual and bicultural. In the political science course, I hoped to pursue my pet topic: the budgetary processes of international organizations. I'd already written, at Carleton University, an essay on the UN's budgetary process; now I hoped to research an essay on the EEC's, the European Economic Community's. I'd learned to dress the part of a jet-setting civil servant. When I stepped off the plane in Geneva, I was wearing a grey three-piece suit. Who could have guessed I was only nineteen? Or the effect I would have on Anand.

It was early Sunday morning but he also wore a suit. His shoes looked handmade, likely Italian. His tie was silk. He was about forty-seven and, like me, he looked fit. He had my father's high forehead but not his broad shoulders. Anand was of slight build like me; we looked like father and son. In the years I'd lived with my father he'd driven only Fords – the '58 Fairlane and '63 Meteor used, the '69 Galaxy new. Anand drove a Mercedes coupe, silver-blue. As a woman had once quipped in a TV commercial for the Ford LTD, the Mercedes looked great on him.

And he wasn't a spy after all. He worked for a bank called Inter-Maritime that financed ships. In the late 1960s or early 1970s, its founding partners had learned about a certain penniless engineer who knew much about ships. The partners had taken him on, and he'd risen to the rank of vice-president. His specialty was Southeast Asia. I knew all this from my father, who in turn had learned it in letters from Geneva. It didn't explain the 3D postcard from Moscow, though. "I was looking into the possibility of shipping Russian grain," Anand said. And I said, "Of course." He pointed out his bank while driving the long way from the airport to his house. The bank stood on a quay on the north shore of Lake Geneva. The house was in a suburb called Vandoeuvres. Here the houses stood farther apart than in the city. Anand's was at the end of a lane bordering a meadow.

After parking the Mercedes in a garage, he led me through what he called "our small chalet." It was a two-storey, four-bedroom house with a finished basement. My father and I had always lived in apartments or on one floor of a house.

But this is how I planned to live one day: with a living room filled with art, the statues kept safe from dust in glass cases; with my own study, its walls lined with built-in bookshelves. Most of the art here was Japanese. The stoneware tea set I'd brought for my aunt would look too North American – too rustic – in this so-called chalet.

We found my aunt in the backyard. It was landscaped like a Japanese garden. Towards one side was a rolling hill balanced on the other side by a stone lantern. The edges of the garden were unfinished, but someone had piled flagstones in a corner near the garage. My aunt looked nothing like the geisha dolls in the living room; I would never have cast her as a banker's wife in some Alpine spy novel. She didn't so much walk as shuffle in her heavy shoes, and her hands often strayed to the small of her back. I knew she was older than Anand, but I hadn't expected her to look older. She spoke just enough English for us to converse and just enough French to shop for groceries. I wondered how she managed in cosmopolitan Geneva until I learned that she had everything she needed in Vandoeuvres.

I met my cousin, Shinobu, in his TV room. He was seventeen or eighteen, just a year or two younger than me. He had a round face unlike mine or Anand's. Shinobu barely spoke to me but later, when we went to the Old Town for a lavish dinner of Peking duck, he made up for it. He spoke more than his parents did, as if having to make up for their silent acceptance of waiting an hour and a half for dinner. I didn't know why they hadn't ordered ahead, but I suspected that Shinobu had chosen the restaurant at the last minute in order to impress me. After an hour he ordered deep-fried rolls, nothing like the eggrolls I'd eaten before. These were long and flaky and so filling that, when the duck finally arrived – first the soup, then the skin, then the meat – we were too full to appreciate it. I didn't see the bill; I only saw a wad of notes pass from Anand to one of our three waiters. This is also how I planned to live, but now I knew something important: one should order ahead for Peking duck.

That evening I repacked my luggage. Whatever I needed for my upcoming tour of Switzerland and Austria would fit in my knapsack. Whatever else I would need for my six weeks in Paris – including the grey suit – went into my soft-sided, green suitcase. This was Anand's idea. He could see that I hadn't travelled alone before and knew little about managing luggage. While repacking, I discovered that I'd lost my recent income tax refund. I'd carried the cheque onto my Swiss Air flight in the bag holding the stoneware tea set. "It'll turn up," Anand said and I believed him. There was something about him: the fact that he knew so much, and not just about travelling, that made me feel at ease; at home in a way my own home had never been reassuring. He planned to take the suitcase with him the next day to Paris, because he had a meeting there. He would leave it for me at a hotel called the George V. When I asked if the suitcase would be safe, he said, "Don't worry. They know me there." Three weeks later, on my first day of class, I would discover that the George V was listed in guidebooks as "somewhat exclusive."

On Monday I woke late and found a note on my door. It was the door to the basement guest room, which was as large as the living room above. Anand expected to return from Paris on Tuesday evening. I should treat his house as my own. So, I did. When I couldn't find an outlet for my electric razor in the downstairs bathroom, I went upstairs. No one seemed to be about. Shinobu was at school; my aunt was likely in her almost Japanese garden.

She and Anand had separate bedrooms. It surprised me and yet it didn't. During the few years my mother had lived with my father and me, she'd also had her own room; sometimes she'd even shared mine. At least my uncle and aunt lived under the same roof. I peeked into her room but didn't enter. At the opposite end of the hallway was Anand's room, which I did enter. The closet door was open. The rack was full of suits, with dozens of silk ties on special hangers. The closet floor was covered with shoes. I finally knew what people meant when they said someone owned fifty pairs of shoes. This was also how I planned to live, but I would manage with fewer shoes. I entered Anand's bathroom and plugged in my razor. Although I'm right-handed, I always shave the left side of my face first. The bathroom door, still open, was also on my left. I'd just finished that side of my face when I heard a sound. My aunt stood outside the door with her hand over her mouth. When I switched off the razor, she lowered her hand and her eyes.

"I am sorry," she said. "I thought my husband changed his mind about going to Paris. Then I saw you and thought it was him." Turning to move away from the door, she said, "You are so much like him when we met."

⇥⫶⇤

ANAND RETURNED from Paris on Tuesday evening. My aunt, Shinobu, and I had finished our quick dinner of fish and rice. Shinobu did homework in his TV room. My aunt went outside and circled the garden. She would stop when she found an especially pleasing view of the lantern and the hill. Anand, still in his good trousers and dress shoes, started setting flagstones on the unfinished border. I felt that I had to earn my keep, so I helped him. Before long my arms grew tired and I wished I'd been less thoughtful. Then Shinobu came outside. When he saw me perspiring, he lent a hand. Now Anand and my aunt watched while Shinobu and I carried the stones together – they were that heavy. After we finished, my aunt thanked us. Shinobu shrugged as if to say it was nothing, then returned to his homework and TV.

"Do you drink?" Anand asked me. "Come, have one if you do."

He led me back through the living room into the front hall and opened what I'd thought was a closet door. It revealed a narrow wooden staircase that led to a panelled attic. At one end stood the bar; at the other end stood wooden shelves covered with miniature liqueur bottles. I picked up a blue and white ceramic house that I knew was from KLM. Anand noticed my amazement at such a collection.

"I used to entertain quite a bit," he said, "but I stopped after they removed one of my kidneys. I travel first class, of course, so I still collect these. Have one. They're good with coffee."

"I don't really drink that much," I said. What I meant was, "I like to drink, but I don't because I can't afford it." I put the KLM house back and moved to look at the cabinet he was opening behind the bar. Tall bottles of liquor, most of them unopened, packed the cabinet. He took a squat bottle out of the fridge and poured a bubbly crimson liquid into a glass. This was my first taste of Campari.

Anand and I sat in padded swivel chairs. Looking as if he were hiding a surprise, he sipped a soda. "This is the first time I've seen you," he said, "so my wife and I would like to give you a gift."

"Can I have your car?" I asked. We both laughed.

"I'll leave it to you in my will," he joked. Then he said something that should have been left unsaid: "If things had turned out differently, all of this would have been yours one day. A boy like you deserves to live well." To dispel our embarrassment – and all the other, unspoken regrets – he went on. "You plan to travel before your classes, you said. I'll give you a choice. You can have as much money as that cheque you mislaid on the plane—"

I must have looked surprised. I certainly felt surprised. The cheque had been for three hundred dollars. But the real surprise was yet to come.

"—or," he said, "I can arrange the next two weeks for you through my travel agent. You can go first class and stay in good hotels. Apparently you're keen on seeing Salzburg – something to do with Mozart, your father says – but have you considered Vienna? I know of some nice hotels there."

I refused the second offer, though I didn't explain why. My final two years with my father – my grades eleven and twelve in Vancouver – had taught me about poverty. Not simply the lack of money but the lack of hope. Only my father's determination and my own luck had ensured that I'd finished high school and entered university. My first two years at Carleton, then a Marxist hotbed, had taught me about class conflict. I didn't intend to compromise my principles too soon, and so I chose the three hundred dollars.

"Is that all?" he asked. "You'll have it tomorrow." Later, I would learn from my father that my choosing the smaller gift had impressed Anand. Why, I wasn't sure.

When he returned from work the next day, he called me into his study and handed me an envelope stuffed with Swiss francs. I spent half of it on the first real camera I'd bought – a clumsy, Russian Zenit – and the rest during my travels sampling what I considered exotic foods: fondue and escargots. I took a photo of Anand. Since I hadn't learned to use the camera properly, the photo didn't turn out. I would spend my two weeks in Berne, Interlaken, and Salzburg at pensions. Or at cheap hotels where maids ironed the sheets instead of washing them. He wouldn't have approved; but, like other students, I assumed that people who travelled first class were bores.

Anand was different, of course; I knew he'd worked hard and added the devil's luck to his own talent. This was the main thing we had in common beyond our ambition and our taste: we were both incredibly lucky men.

I spent the rest of the week touring Geneva and trying to make friends with Shinobu. Once we even watched a movie on TV, a space adventure called *Marooned* dubbed in French. Like *Captain Hornblower*, it starred Gregory Peck. Perhaps Shinobu was only shy, but he rebuffed all my attempts at friendship. Brotherhood appeared out of the question although, on both sides of my family, cousins considered themselves brothers and sisters. He attended a polytechnic with students from around the world and seemed glad to talk about his plans. After graduating, he planned to study engineering, then business, then join the bank. "My father's bank." I changed the subject to the two-wheeled *velos* I'd seen in Geneva traffic and asked why he didn't have one. "Why should I?" he said. "I'll have a car soon." I didn't own a car, and few people I knew in university owned one. The more annoyed I felt with him, the more I wondered what twist of fate had made me my father's son instead of Anand's son. It wasn't a fair thought, but I was only nineteen and those days I thought – no, I was sure – that life has to be fair.

THE EVENING BEFORE I left Geneva, I stayed in the kitchen after dinner to speak to my aunt. I would remember our conversation almost word for word in years to come. I'd grown up with a gift, the aural equivalent of a photographic memory. But more than this, I would remember the conversation because it was the only real one we had. I wanted to thank her for her hospitality.

"Oh, it is nothing," she said.

"No, it was really nice of you," I insisted. "We've never met, but you treated me like one of the family."

"You are one of the family," she said. "Besides, we met once before. Was it fifteen years ago? I saw you in Bombay. Perhaps you were too young to remember?"

"I remember now," I said, and it was true: I did. "You came down to the lobby in an old-fashioned elevator."

"And you were with your mother at the time," my aunt said. "You and Shinobu are very close in that way. Just like him, you did not see your father for many years because he was away making a better life for you. But now you and your father are together again. We are all together again." She stopped and stared at the floor. We were sitting on high bar stools at the kitchen counter. Suddenly she smiled, hiding her teeth the way she'd covered her mouth on my first morning in the house. "My husband reads me your father's letters," she said. "You want to be an international civil servant? If you join the United Nations or the Red Cross, you can come here and live with us. Then your father can come to visit. I have not seen him since my marriage. You can take him to Mont Blanc." She pronounced it *Mount Blank.* "You can see the view from the top. I have heard it is very pretty."

"Haven't you been there?" I asked.

"I do not like travelling, except to Japan."

"My father lived in Kyoto," I said. As if she didn't know. "He loved it. Was your father a shipbuilder? Is that how you met my uncle?"

She laughed so hard, she forgot to hide her teeth. Then she said, "My father was killed in the Second World War. He was just a poor soldier. He would never have dreamt I would someday be married to a banker."

Or be living in such a fine house.

The next morning, Anand dropped me at the train station.

He waved and then drove off in his silver-blue Mercedes. I couldn't wave, though, because I was hefting my knapsack onto my back.

4

IN THE LATE SUMMER of 1979, four years later, I started my civil service career. I wasn't with the UN or the Red Cross although I'd become fluent in French and had even studied Russian. I was with the forestry branch of a provincial department in a Canadian prairie town: Prince Albert, Saskatchewan. Early one evening in September, I think, I received a collect call from Geneva. It was from my father.

He'd flown to Switzerland at my aunt's request. Anand had been suffering from cancer for the past three years. He'd hidden it from everyone except my aunt. Only a week before, he'd suffered a heart attack while shopping and had died before the ambulance could arrive. He hadn't even turned fifty-two. The bank had given its employees a morning off. Everyone had stood on the quay to watch my father immerse Anand's ashes in the lake. My father told me all this woodenly. There was more, though – much more – which I pieced together in the years following Anand's death. Much of it involved Shinobu's failure to follow in Anand's footsteps; yet much of it came from my father – whose opinion of other young men had never been as high as his opinion of himself as a young man.

REGINA, CHRISTMAS 1994:

As often happens during the holiday season, my thoughts went to my extended family, and lingered fondly on my Uncle Ananda.

It was now nearly twenty years since I saw him for the first and last time. Half a dozen suits hang in my closet with a handful of silk ties, and I wear sandals, not shoes. This is ironic because my father-in-law sells shoes, but a weak back won't allow me to wear anything with heels. Like Anand's father-in-law, mine also went to war, but he fought on the right side, and he came back. Like Anand, I'm one of the few people in my family to marry a non-Indian. I also married a woman who is slightly older than me. But unlike Anand's wife, whose name I think is Kimiko, though no one seems to remember, Shelley looked younger than me. Much younger. Like them, we lost our first child; unlike them, we couldn't have another. And, like them, we lived at some distance from our families – on both sides.

As for our car, we'd bought it for a dollar from Shelley's brother. Before that, it belonged to their grandfather, a farmer. It's a '68 Ford we called Old Blue as if it was from a prairie joke about cowboys. Or from a western starring Randolph Scott. Shelley knew that, some days, I would rather be driving a Mercedes coupe from Switzerland into France; that I wished I could stay at hotels with names like George V, which should properly be pronounced *Georges Cinq*. But we never spoke about such things because we knew each other too well. I believe I was everything to her and, while I'm not a man who gives way easily to sentiment, not after all that I've seen, both here in Canada and abroad – she was the light of my life.

EXTENDED FAMILIES

My Aunt Kimiko and Uncle Ananda.

SOMEWHERE IN THE U.S., a young man lives far from his family. True, he lives with his immediate family – his wife and child – but he often thinks of his larger, extended family: people he's had no contact with for years.

His father was the youngest son of an Indian engineer, his mother the daughter of a Japanese soldier killed in the war. Their marriage was not arranged. They met in Yokohama while the father was in the Indian merchant marine. He used his earnings to purchase a flat in Bombay that he never got to live in. Now he accepted a transfer to London, a management position, then lost his job due to circumstances beyond his control. Their first child died. The second survived.

The merchant mariner grew poor. He returned to India only once, when his own father lay dying. His wife and son lived in Osaka, Japan, with what remained of her own family. Her husband returned to sea but never admitted hardship until forced to seek help from his favourite brother: to adopt the boy should the need arise.

There proved no such need. The mariner's reputation as a man who knew ships reached a Swiss bank. It hired him to approve the plans of ships it financed. Since most of these were built in the Far East, his knowledge of Japanese and of the Japanese proved useful. His wife and son left Osaka. Even as the boy finished primary school, his father became a vice-president.

The mother kept a house in Geneva; the boy attended a *polytechnique*; the father drove a Mercedes-Benz. Yet they rarely entertained. The mother wouldn't have known what to say. Chocolates and watches, yes, but Geneva was famous for other things: a lake, a lagoon, a fountain. Swans.

No one in the father's extended family asked the boy, "Are you happy?" He was part Indian, part Japanese, born in London, raised in uncertainty. He could no more play the banker's son than his mother could play the banker's wife. It was said he took refuge in drugs, but those who claimed such things were the members of this extended family who were prone to passing judgment.

His father sent him to a private college in the U.S. It expelled him. By now his father was himself dying. Not of old age; he was fifty-one. He was dying of cancer, but it was his heart that failed him. One day he stopped at a pharmacy for his medicine. The last words he heard were French: "*Calmez-vous.*" Not even, "*Calme-toi.*"

What of the boy: the young man? He blamed everyone except himself. To stop him from squandering his father's wealth, his mother called on the uncle, her husband's favourite brother. The uncle issued orders. The young man rebelled. At last, it was said, he entered a clinic to seek help. Everyone congratulated the uncle. He congratulated himself. While at the clinic, the young man made a friend. She too was from a wealthy family. Greek, it was said. She too was misunderstood, and neither had close friends. He didn't marry her, though. He married someone else, an American. They live far from the family that never thought to ask, "Are you happy?" While playing with his child, he often thinks of the family he once had.

SOMEWHERE IN SWITZERLAND, a woman lives alone. Over a decade has passed since her husband's ashes were immersed in Lake Geneva. During afternoon walks, she ignores the banks on the opposite quay. Barely glances at the floral clock. Near the fountain in the lagoon, she loses track of time. If asked, she says, "I like to think...my husband swims with the swans." Few people ask. It embarrasses them: her uncertain English, Berlitz French, the unforgiving Japanese.

PART TWO

What Am I Doing Here?

My paternal grandmother, Bhagirathi, with Rakosh and Anand in Bangalore.

The House on Debur Road

Sunday, October 9, 1977

GRANDMA WAKES ME at 4:30 a.m. to catch train number 222, the
Mysore Mail. Go outside at 6:00 to find an auto (an autorickshaw). Not much traffic; just the odd bicycle and occupied
auto. There's a glow in the east but the sun hasn't yet risen. Finally get an auto. We load my suitcase and flight bag and a
smaller flight bag. Holds a toaster along with an electric fan –
twice as heavy as my own back in Ottawa – both for my father.
After many years in Canada, he has finally returned to India
and is teaching at the National Institute of Engineering in
Mysore. I reach the station at 6:15. A long wait, which I spend
in the "reservation car"; finally the Mysore train leaves. Try to
read Nehru's *Glimpses of World History* but give up; I'm too tired
to read. Across from me sits a plump woman in her late twenties. Wears a blue sari with bangles, a necklace and earrings.
Beside me sits a lanky young man. We don't speak till the train
reaches Mysore. Turns out he's a TV technician at a racecourse
(a racetrack). Am being stared at by other passengers who have
labelled me a foreigner. During the whole journey, a group of
young men sing; play accordion and drum.

The country we pass is rich land planted with rice – in
places the knee-high shoots are bright yellow-green in the

sun – and sugar cane. The rivers run orange but near Mysore they're a dirty green. For about an hour we pass rocky hills that look like those Indian temples that are carved from a single rock. At one station, on the other side of the train, a beggar thrusts his crippled left arm through the grille. With his right hand, he holds out a bowl for money. At another station, a small hunchback looks up from his feet as the train pulls in. Instead of begging at the windows, he picks a half-smoked cigarette off the ground, perches on a stone bench, and smokes. The train passes women drying clothes on the grassy banks of creeks and rivers. Striped and coloured saris spread out like carpets under the sun.

Appa is at Mysore Railway Station to meet me. He looks little different from last Christmas (when I saw him in Lillooet, B.C., where he was working for a private company); but he dresses appropriately for here: with his shirt tail out and an umbrella hooked on one arm. We chat while having coffee.

We buy a one-month ticket for me between Nanjangud and Mysore, then board the local train. I tell him about the musical young men. He describes the mad rush for seats and the crowding on local trains; says the main culprits are students. He points out a two-storey house my grandfather built during their stay in Mysore during Appa's childhood and youth. South of Mysore is a large hill with a temple on it. And a palace converted into a hotel. For a while the land is bare, but after we cross a large river the land is again covered with crops.

Nanjangud looks small but has about fifty thousand people. It's called a town. I see only the road from the railway station to a traffic circle and the road west out of town. We pick up two bicycles being watched at a cycle shop by a young boy. Load the luggage on the bicycles and Appa leaves to buy some food. I sit on a folding wooden chair that the boy brings out for me. Feel strange in my sandals with socks, tucked-in shirt, English country cap. We start walking the bicycles out of town. Appa has so much trouble with the toaster and heavy fan that he hires a local cab to carry my luggage. The cab is a two-wheeled, brightly coloured carriage drawn by a horse with a mangy coat. Real cabs are for trips to Mysore or to Ooty (Ootacamund, a hill station), not for short trips.

I'm left to follow the cart while Appa stops to buy bread. The horse is too uncoordinated to gallop properly; trots as if it has four left hooves. A fifteen-minute ride brings us to the house that Appa's renting, one of the few concrete houses for miles around. A boy, the son of the watchman on this farm, hangs about the house with nothing to do. The house is locked and I look into the verandah: there are two cane armchairs and a metal teapoy (a coffee table). Through the grille of a window, I look into the main room or living room. It's practically bare.

Appa arrives and pays the driver. Appa's very proficient at arguing in Kannada, the local language. He unlocks the verandah doors and we go inside.

What have I got myself into? What am I doing here?

THE HOUSE IS a two-bedroom affair but the living room is also used as a bedroom. It contains the only bed, a cabinet with glass doors set into the wall, a stand-up closet or wardrobe with a half mirror, and a table with a short-wave radio covered with a cloth. Stretching to the right is a hallway and off this are a large, bare kitchen; an Indian bathing room with two buckets of water and a coiled immersion heater; and an Indian-style latrine – a ceramic-lined hole in the ground with a ceramic pan around it and two ceramic footrests – and a brass vessel of water for washing. There's also one large room that the owners use as a storeroom. No furniture in either of the bedrooms. In one are my things; in the other are Appa's and his bedroll; he'll be sleeping here during my stay, while I sleep in his bed in the other bedroom. In the kitchen are two hot plates, a shelf of dishes – stainless steel and china – and some pans of water. Appa keeps containers of food in the pans so that ants can't attack the bread and jam. In the bathroom are two buckets of water and a coiled immersion heater. Water comes from a well behind the house.

There's only one way to settle into a place like this: I use the latrine right away. The hard part for Appa is keeping his balance while squatting. The hard part for me isn't keeping my balance; it's washing my behind with water from a brass vessel. After using the latrine, I put on the dhoti Appa gives me. Allows for more circulation of air around the legs than trousers do. He cooks an omelette for lunch. While I eat, he talks about the lazy watchman and his wife and son. They live in a brick hut with a tiled roof behind us, on the other side of the well. Appa seems to have a great dislike for the local people, especially what he calls their "cheating methods." Takes it all quite seriously.

We sit in the verandah. It's surrounded on three sides by waist-high walls topped by grille-work, like the wire playground fences back home. There are clouds in the west and suddenly the sun appears, yellow-orange. Disappears in a few minutes. You can hear crickets chirping, grey owls screeching, the sound of wind passing through the young coconut palms in front of the house. The noise is like falling rain. You can also hear the passing of bullock carts and buses on the paved road, about twenty-five yards north of the house.

While we're preparing for bed, Appa chases a lizard about five inches long into the bedroom and hits it with a broom.

He carries the stunned lizard outside. When I enter the bedroom, I find the lizard's tail, red where it was joined to the body, still writhing on the floor. They drop their tails when they panic. So ends my first day in my father's new house. I force myself to laugh about it all. Get an idea for a story about a young Canadian woman who marries an Indian and comes to a place like this dreaming of romance.

My paternal grandmother, Bhagirathi, with me, aged three, in Mauritius in 1959.

Appa, My Father

Friday, September 30, 1977

1: Fratricide

A POET ONCE TOLD ME, "All sons kill their fathers." This poet knew much about such things. His own father died young, shot in the back late one night at his desk. Not by the poet. And he was not the sort of man who went through life guarding his own back. We met over ten years ago, when he settled in Saskatchewan with another poet. Even then I saw myself in him: the same love of beauty and truth, the same impatience with fools.

He gave me hope without trying. That's the best kind; the kind of hope that goes deep. I was watching his poetry class once, marvelling at the loving impatience in his voice, at the beauty he could impart to even technical words: form, ghazal, villanelle; imagistic, lyric; caesura; masculine rhyme, feminine rhyme, paradigm; closure. Words I even now don't understand: sounds to be savoured. "The only thing that separates me from him is twenty years," I thought. "If I care about writing as much as he does, if I pursue it with his single-mindedness..." Twenty years, give or take a few: only that.

Later, we discovered that I was nearly as old as his eldest

son. He laughed in amusement and shock, for he had forgotten that he was already middle-aged. In jest I called him Dad, and he called me Son. We became as a father and son should be once the son learns that life is full of betrayals. We were friends.

We even had similar dreams. Mine was to finish the basement in the house that my wife Shelley and I owned, a house we bought from these two poets. His dream was to build a greenhouse in their new backyard. Reality had forced us, he and I, to lower our sights. Not for our writing; those remained often impossibly high. We lowered our sights on life. But to say that we were like father and son is misleading, for I have never wanted to kill him.

My father and I are not friends. In the twelve years between my two visits to India, in the 1970s and 1980s, I have seen him only three times: once for three weeks, once for a week, once for a day and a half, all on his visits to Canada. Just over a month in twelve years. I often wanted to kill him. I no longer do. It's not simply that I have forgiven him. There is that. I no longer want to kill him because I discovered how easy it would be.

We were at my Uncle Nagasha's house in Mysore. Nagasha commented on how much my father resembled my grandfather. I secretly refused to believe it. I admired my grandfather. I could afford to, because I hadn't known him well. He hadn't raised me; my father had. He was standing to one side while Nagasha and his wife posed for my camera. Suddenly it struck me: how old my father looked. How frail. I could have broken his neck with one hand. Or that's how it seemed. Better yet, I could have closed one hand on his throat and slammed his head against a wall. Of course I did neither. But in that instant, his hold on me fell away. The father I had known was dead. At last.

Until that moment, whenever I remembered him as he once had been, I remembered the bad things first. Now I try to remember the good. And perhaps because I learned to remember them so late, they remain with me now. It took twenty-seven years, from the time I was six until nearly thirty-three, to forgive him. Twenty-seven years, give or take a few: only that.

I will not grieve for my father when he dies. I will grieve for the man he could have been.

2: *Promises*

MY MOTHER WORKS in Toronto and I live with my father in Ottawa, where he works for the National Research Council. "He will take good care of you," she promised. She promised that for three years while we waited in India to join him. I call him Appa, which means father in his mother tongue, but I don't think of him as Appa. I met him only once before she left me with him. His visit to India, two years before, was a quick one. As quickly, I forgot him. I was only four then. Now I am six.

He is cooking supper, omelette again. Eggs congealed around onion and tomato, diced. In India I tasted eggs only once. Our servant, Mary, boiled an egg because my mother wanted me to learn Canadian ways. The experiment was not a success. Here we have omelettes every second night. One night, I rebel.

"If you don't eat, you'll fall ill," he says. I refuse. He slams the table and shouts, "Eat!" I begin to cry. I get down from my chair and sit on the floor with my back to the wall. That was how we ate in India but only on special occasions. He rises with my plate, sets it on the floor, and crouches in front of me. He is a large man with a thick neck and hairy arms. He cannot abide it when I cry.

He grabs my throat with his left hand, shoves my head back against the wall. His palm presses into my throat. My hair scritches between my scalp and the wall. He begins shovelling omelette into my mouth. I am six going on seven, but I know: I can either eat or choke.

He leaves the plate on the floor, rises and backs away. This is not the man my mother promised would take good care of me. "You're not my father!" I scream. I am only six, but I know, and I tell him again: "You are not my father."

3: Sportsmanship

Try to avoid questions that begin with "why."

— Family Ties That Bind

MY FATHER ONCE played cricket against what later became the Pakistan National Team. He was playing slip, I think; the most difficult spot: near the batsman but off to the side. The batsman up was their best. He could hit centuries, a hundred runs, and he made only one mistake that day. He nicked the ball and my father lunged. He missed. When he tells this story, he shakes his head.

Another time, my father's team was playing away. The host team arranged lunch, ordered out from a nearby hotel. By mid-afternoon, my father's team forfeited the match. Food poisoning. When he tells this story, he always laughs.

I am seven. Civil service teams play cricket on the grounds of Rideau Hall, the Governor General's mansion. In the pavilion, a wooden building with secretive changing rooms, is a soft drink machine. Bottles hang from rows of slots, different flavours in different slots. Pure Spring ginger ale, cream soda, lemon lime. Move a bottle down its slot and into the gate. Feed in a dime and pull up. I always choose

Orange Crush. Even now it tastes of green pavilions, cricket whites, mothers on the lawn in folding chairs, cries of "Well caught!" Orange Crush is cricket.

On the way home after a match, my father says the governor general invited him to tea but my father declined. "Georges Vanier?" I ask. "We could have had tea with Georges Vanier, and you turned him down?" My father says, "I couldn't very well go in my cricketing clothes." Later I boast, "I nearly had tea with Georges Vanier."

I am nine. My father has been trying to teach me cricket for two years. We are on the grounds of RMC, the Royal Military College, and I am tiring of his orders. I want to have fun and he is making me do drills. My cheeks feel as red as the hard leather ball he bowls. Finally I throw down my bat. "I am not learning cricket!" I declare. He slaps me. Only once. But hard.

I am twenty-five. He is spending the summer with me in Regina, in my second-floor walk-up near the tracks. A suite too small for a father and son. I ask a question unasked for sixteen years: "Why did you hit me that time I said I didn't want to learn cricket?"

He looks up from a book. "What are you talking about?" he asks.

"You always hit me for every little thing," I say, "but that time you hit me so hard. Why?"

He says, "That's the way we were brought up. I didn't know any better." He goes back to his book while I fume. "At any rate," he adds without looking up, "I never once hit you on a cricket pitch. That would have been poor sportsmanship."

4: Moving Days

I NEVER LEARNED to play the piano because I couldn't practise at home. Even if we could have afforded a piano, we wouldn't have had one. We moved every year, often within the same city. For a while our living room furniture was patio furniture because it was easy to assemble, disassemble, reassemble. Our addresses during the eleven years I lived with my father:

610 Montreal Road, Ottawa, in what was then called Eastview and is now called Vanier. I don't remember the apartment number. I attend Ashbury College, an exclusive school not meant for families in Eastview. My father hires a man to wax the hardwood floor when we move out. He dislikes leaving traces.

50 Selkirk Avenue, yet another apartment in Eastview but closer to the river, to Ottawa proper. I buy comic books at a corner store, the Busy Bee. Lorna Going, my baby sitter's granddaughter, tries to teach me to fish, with little success. She takes me to *Mary Poppins*, and for weeks we sing: Supercalifragilisticexpialidocious.

He has no idea what it means.

Bowling Green One, Kingston, on the corner of Bath Road and Sir John A. Macdonald Boulevard. They are always digging basements for new buildings. In winter, boys and girls skate on the frozen holes; in spring, we pole rafts made of boards meant to keep us out. My father can't get tenure at RMC because he doesn't have his doctorate.

Then a basement apartment that he lives in while I go back to Ashbury, this time as a boarder. In spring, the basement floods. Most of his belongings, packed in boxes, escape damage. Still, he vows never to live in a basement again. He doesn't have to: I decide I prefer public schools. They seem more real.

Another building on Sir John A., across from the Kingston Shopping Centre with its Bad Boy furniture store. This is the year he begins finding fault with everything I do. The year a neighbour, Mrs. Farrell, gives me lunch when I come home from school. The year he takes me to New York City for Christmas. We stay at the YMCA. One night I go to the bathroom down the hall and pass a drunk. He is sawing the round wooden ornament off a banister. I don't ask why.

Building J off Westgate Drive, Bethlehem, Pennsylvania. The year I learn to play baseball and my father finally earns his doctorate at Lehigh University. At last. The year I play the baritone at Nitschmann Junior High. The year I learn this song:

B-e-t-h-l-e-h-e-m spells Bethlehem!
Proud of all the years she's been a city.
Fifty years!
That is why we sing this pretty ditty.
Give her a cheer!
B-e-t-h-l-e-h-e-m so grand.
She's the town of renown,
Christmas City in the U.S.A.,
Bethlehem, give her a hand!

Bowling Green Three, Kingston. I may have forgotten Two; I'm sure we lived there as well. This will be the longest we live in any one city at one time: three years. We make trips to Algonquin Park and Expo '67: "Man and His World." My father's health grows worse from the dampness and cold, the long hours in his lab. I grow moody, so he makes me take up sailing, join air cadets. Anything to get me out of the house.

One Thursday in August, when I am fifteen, he comes home and asks, "Do you have any library books out?" I always have library books out. "Take them back," he says. "We're leaving for Vancouver on Monday. I've quit my job." And so we pack up the car and drive. He drives. I remember the sunset on the lake at Ignace, Ontario. He curses while he unloads the patio furniture from the car in Ignace, west of Thunder Bay, and repacks it to send by train. Our car, a Ford

Galaxy, was only two years old, but the weight of the furniture had been slowing it down.

The forests north of Superior. Bison at the zoo in Winnipeg. The sunset at Grenfell, Saskatchewan. In Calgary he says, "What river is that?" I want to say, "Fucked if I know." Instead I say, "Beats me," and he grows annoyed. "This is your chance to learn about Canada," he says. And then the mountains, oh the mountains, the gondola up Mount Norquay near Banff, Peyto Lake on the way to Jasper. Imagine: a lake that changes colour throughout the day. We see it as turquoise. Then down past the Premier range of mountains of B.C. and past the whirlpool at Hell's Gate. I remember the motel at Hope, a chalet. How he keeps repeating the name Hope to lift my spirits. And his. Our first night in Vancouver at the YMCA. No drunk sawing at banisters here. Just a question mark after the Y.

Two last addresses, in Vancouver:

A highrise on Alma Street near Broadway. Nights lying awake listening to the fountain in front. The beginnings of insomnia. Eighteen years of insomnia. Evenings spent alone walking in the rain to the library while he attends night class at teachers' college. Other evenings in the army cadets. His idea again: anything to keep me out of the house. He begins talking about returning to India. I lay plans for escape.

The 3800 block of Fourth Avenue West. When the caretaker, Mr. Kostiniuk, falls ill, my father burns the garbage for him. For ten dollars a week. Mrs. Kostiniuk bakes loaves of round bread for us, slips a dollar bill to me with each one. Then he gets a job, part-time, but a job. Spends his first fifty dollars on a sports jacket and trousers at the Army and Navy. A flashy yellow jacket to fit his new mood. But he leaves his wallet in the changing room and returns to find it gone. He still pays for the clothes, later, but he never wears that jacket.

The following August, I leave for university in the east. Back in Ottawa. Swear I will never go home again. Of course I do.

And in the ten years between my first apartment and finally buying a house, I live in eleven different places: Ottawa (three), Saskatoon and Prince Albert (one each), Regina (six). But I promise myself two things. Real wooden furniture. And a piano. Much of our furniture is second hand, but it is wood. Even the piano is second hand, refinished by a friend from pink Roxatone to its original oak veneer. Someday, I will learn to play it.

My graduating studio photograph at Carleton University in April of 1977.

LOCAL COLOUR

Monday, October 10, 1977

APPA WAKES ME at eight. Cooks me a breakfast of a fried egg, two slices of bread with ghee (clarified butter that doesn't have to be refrigerated) and jam, and milk. A milkman brings this milk twice daily, then it's boiled for drinking or making curds. Appa leaves for work: a trip of more than an hour, first bicycling to the station in Nanjangud, then travelling by steam train to Mysore. I catch up on the last few days' entries in this journal. I've fallen behind, and there was no time to catch up in the evenings because electric lights attract flying insects. Then I walk west along Debur Road.

The land on either side is used for rice paddies. The rice is either knee-high or being planted as young shoots by groups of women. They chat loudly while they work, bent over. Elsewhere, one farmer digs up mud with a bent, spade-like tool while another pats the mud into a paddy wall with his foot. White birds – some form of crane or heron – stalk the paddies. Overhead fly crows and what looks like a vulture because of the widely separated feathers of its wings. In one irrigation ditch, a man washes his bicycle. In another a boy washes himself. About a mile west of the house is Debur Village, and the paved road curves north and then west around this village for the benefit of buses. From this bend in the road I walk back without entering the village itself. Even here I see a young – mid-twenties – woman dressed well in a clean sari and blouse and her hair oiled. Fancy earrings. Most of the people wear tattered short pants and T-shirts. Or old white dhotis, which they tuck up to reveal old, coloured boxer shorts. Many of the children, the littlest ones, go naked. Hardly anyone wears sandals, and those who do don't wear socks. Neither do I now.

See and hear lots of flying insects on the way back. Small, blue-green butterflies that fly in twos or threes. Dragonflies with red bodies: two flying attached, head to tail, with one humped over the other. Must be practising their *Kama Sutra*. Large butterflies, almost the size of hummingbirds, fly too fast for a close look. Butterflies with red wings that have black and white borders. The insects plaguing the house are wasps and ants. In the living room, I discover a column of ants, follow the column, and find the ants hauling away the carcass of a spider. The wasps build nests everywhere: in light switches, nail holes. I don't like them. They come too close to us in the verandah. By late afternoon I take refuge under the mosquito net of my bed.

Write a long, closely spaced letter to Jacquie M. about India and this house; then, still wearing my dhoti, cycle to Nanjangud to meet Appa, coming home from work. We have sodas at the cycle shop. These are no more than carbonated water and fruit syrup and are supposed to be good for the stomach. The bottles are Indian ones of thick glass. In the narrow neck is a marble, which rises to block the mouth when the carbon dioxide reaches a certain pressure. The bottles are opened by the vendor. He uses a short spike inside a metal cup, which fits snugly over the top, and pounds once with his fist to free the marble.

We have mutton for supper. Appa fries it in a pan with eggplant and onions. It's my first meat in ten days. While we eat, we're kept company by countless insects that fly around the verandah light, then by a grasshopper that's become trapped in the house. After dark, the verandah doors are kept closed to keep out rats, which infest the lean-to behind the house. In the distance, lightning flashes but we hear no thunder. We can see a lot: the lights of Nanjangud to the east and Debur to the west; also, north of us and south of Mysore, the lights of a village called Kalaley and lights on the large hill with the temple (Chamundi Hill). On the shortwave radio we listen to Beethoven's Fifth Symphony, playing on Radio Moscow.

THE FIRST HOMEOPATH

Tuesday, October 11, 1977

GO TO MYSORE with Appa. The station at Nanjangud is crowded with students and so, after the train pulls in, we throw some books we're carrying through the open window onto a pair of seats to claim then, then join the crowd entering the carriage. From one of the south suburban stations of Mysore, we walk to the National Institute of Engineering, also known as NIE. Along the way, Appa points out touch-me-not plants, whose leaves fold in half when touched. While we walk, he talks, mainly complaining about local attitudes and conditions. The students are on strike today, so he stops to ask a police officer whether any trouble is expected. None is. At the entrance to NIE are purple and red bougainvillaea.

Later, I open an account at the nearby Syndicate Bank, and Appa walks in with my cousin Radha's brother-in-law, Ranghanathan. He is younger than her husband, Jagadish. The three of us have coffee in Appa's office, a large bare room that he shares with someone else. After coffee, he and I go to a nearby market by bus and here we visit a woman doctor, a homeopath, about my chronically bad skin. He says that I've tried everything else all these years and yet it's still dry and itches and cracks open. Asks me to trust him. The doctor's in her late forties and has bad teeth. She asks questions, deletes certain foods like ghee from my diet, and gives me medicine that looks like small white sugar pills. Her office is exposed to the street, with a half wall to protect the doctor and her patients from view. Other patients wait outside, close by, so this means they can see and hear everything. Next we do some shopping and walk quite far, then return to the railway station via the cricket pitch in a *maidan* (a large field).

From Nanjangud we cycle home and then I bathe. I'm sweating heavily and my skin hurts. On Radio Moscow that night is one of my favourite songs, "Hotel California" by The Eagles:

> *You can check out any time you want,*
> *But you can never leave.*

My paternal grandmother, Bhagirathi, with me, aged one-and-a-half, in Mauritius in 1957

A MOST DIFFICULT MAN

My maternal grandfather, Hanuman, a mathematician
who specialized in N-dimensional geometry in projective form.

I HAVE FEW STORIES about my maternal grandfather – my *tathayya* – but I do have heirlooms. I found them in my mother's effects after she died: photographs and a pocket watch. He died before I was born but, according to her stories about him (she told me few), and her bitter references to him (these were many, mainly of how he mistreated my grandmother), he was a most difficult man.

The photographs first. There are five.

In one, my grandfather stands on a seaside walk with his back to the sea. He wears a hat and greatcoat and clutches a walking stick. In another, he sits with two men, all three in Indian clothing: short-sleeved shirts, sarong-like white dhotis, loose cloths draped over their shoulders. They sit on invisible chairs in front of a backdrop: a heavy painted drape pulled back to reveal painted, Italianate trees. Of the three men, only my grandfather doesn't wear a wristwatch.

In yet another photo, marked "May 1947 Lahore" in my mother's hand, he stands alone again, this time in a garden. On the very grounds he walked between delivering lectures? Perhaps. He wears a three-piece suit and keeps his hands clasped behind his back, his eyes stern above a professorial beard.

In my two favourite photos of him, he is trying to smile. The first might have been taken in England, once again posed in front of a backdrop: this time of a painted and panelled study, the books on the shelves also painted. My grandfather, wearing a three-piece suit, is seated in an ornate chair. A pipe smoking gentleman, with a hand on the chair's arm, stands beside him. A brother? My mother's London uncle? In the last photograph, my grandfather finally looks at home. Indeed, he is at home, and it's the only photo I have of him with his wife and children. They're all at Tirumala: that holiest of places in South India; the home of our family god. But even in this photo, as he so often did in his own mind, my grandfather walks ahead of his wife and away from their children.

His name was Chintakindi Hanumanthappa-Rao, Chintakindi his family name, Hanumanthappa-Rao his given name. He would have been named for the god Hanuman and yet it's hard to imagine his ever having been young enough to be called Hanuman; to imagine anyone feeling close enough to call him Hanuman. Most of all, unlike the god, my grandfather doesn't seem to have been lovably clever. Brilliant, yes; demanding, very much so; clever, hardly; lovable, no.

VEN BEGAMUDRÉ

The first Hanuman, the monkey god, is agile and quick. His mother is a monkey queen and his father is the wind. Hanuman has yellow skin that glows like gold and a face as red as ruby. The length of his tail is immeasurable. He can change his size at will, and he can fly. In our Hindu epic, *Ramayana*, Hanuman, with an army of monkeys and bears, helps the god-king Rama rescue his beloved wife Sita from the evil King of Lanka. In return for Hanuman's service, Rama promises him any boon he cares to name. Hanuman asks to live as long as men and women will speak of Rama's deeds. And so Hanuman becomes immortal – because, as long as we keep telling stories, the memory of Rama can never die.

The god Hanuman is also a grammarian; my grandfather Hanuman was a mathematician. In the early 1920s, his family sent him to study in Britain. He learned to dress like a proper Englishman and yet he disliked the British, not because they ruled India but because of his experiences at Cambridge. Future mathematicians at this famous university wrote a set of three exams called the Tripos. According to an age-old tradition, the man who received the highest marks, the senior wrangler, would be carried through the town by his fellow students. But Hanuman's brilliance caused a problem. How could young gentlemen carry an Indian (a Black, as the British called us then) through the streets of an English town? After much debate, Hanuman's fellow students did carry him (it was only sporting that they should), but the incident crystallized his dislike for the British. Or so my mother said. Her sister remembers all of this quite differently: Hanuman did not come first and become the senior wrangler; he passed and became a mere wrangler. But this much is certain: unlike my mother's London uncle, Hanuman returned to India and never again left.

Even so, he was rarely home. He left his wife to raise their four children – two boys, two girls – while he taught mathematics at Lahore University, far away from them all.

Their home was in a town called Visakhapatnam, also called Vizagapatam, more often simply Vizag. It's on the Bay of Bengal and is roughly halfway between Calcutta in the north and Madras in the south. Near Vizag is a second town called Waltair and the two towns are more or less one. Vizag is the business, industrial, and dock area; Waltair is a popular seaside resort more suited to the family of a professor. Vizag-Waltair are in the South Indian state that's now called Andhra Pradesh.

Lahore is inland on the far side of the subcontinent, in Punjab. The five rivers of Punjab don't flow into the Bay of Bengal; they flow into the Arabian Sea. To reach his university, Hanuman had to take the train northwest to Delhi and then to Lahore. It was a distance of some twelve hundred miles as the crow (or the monkey god) flies. He stayed in Lahore all through the school year, living in a hotel, and came home only for summers.

As for the watch I found in my mother's effects, it's a Zenith Prima, Swiss Made by Favre-Leuba & Co. So the face insists, the bold markings black except for the red Zenith. The hours are marked by Roman numerals, the four by four I's and not an IV. The watch has only one hand, the long one that marks minutes. The short hand, which marks hours, is broken. So is the second hand, that is, the hand that marks off seconds. If the watch still worked, this hand would rotate on a small dial nestled at the bottom between the V and the VII. There's no marking for six, no VI. And the numerals for the seconds, in increments of ten, are in Arabic.

Like the man who owned this watch, the watch is extremely efficient. It's not even necessary to open it to tell the time. In the middle of the cover is a circle of convex glass that allows the owner to note the time without having to open the cover. Around this flattened, glass bubble is a second circle of Roman numerals, black on the silver. Here's another thing: except for the crown, which is brass, the rest of the case is silver. It is tarnished and likely hasn't been polished since my grandfather died. On the back is a small shield, suitable for engraving with one's arms or, if one is merely a gentleman, with a monogram. The shield on the back of Hanuman's watch – called in England a half-hunter – is blank.

My mother's only fond memory of him was of the time she took him what she thought was an original theorem. He listened patiently, then explained that the theorem was not original. But he praised her and, in later years, she liked to remember him like this: seated in his study in lamplight and speaking fluent mathematics.

More often, though, she said, "He made her life hell," referring to her mother.

Hanuman died shortly after India became independent in 1947. Something my mother said when I was young puzzled me for years. She said, harshly, "He threw himself into a tank." I pictured a huge, metal tank empty except for a broken, bleeding corpse. But of course she meant an Indian tank, a reservoir. And she told me one other thing: "I gave him his first grandchild, a boy. He would have loved you."

NAGA MEANS SERPENT

Wednesday, October 12, 1977

WE GO TO MYSORE again but this time only to have lunch with Appa's eldest brother, Nagasha – a man named after a serpent god. He's actually my grandfather Krishna's eldest brother's son, whom my grandfather adopted and brought up. First we buy some hardware for installing a sink. On our way to the bus stand, we stop to watch a snake charmer. He's not the half-naked mystic I expected. Has two cobras in flat baskets, kept tied up. He shows off a baby python and a five-foot green and white snake. He keeps up a patter, explains how he caught the snakes, their eating habits. After each phrase an assistant beats a drum or makes an exclamation: "Hah!" The charmer is slow in showing the cobra because the crowd is slow to toss money. We leave. In the autorickshaw on the way to Nagasha's house, Appa warns me that Nagasha's wife is very orthodox. I should not touch any food with my left hand. Should even sit on it if necessary to remember this.

Nagasha's house is in a quiet suburb near the Chamarajapuram Railway Station of Mysore. On the gate, in stone, is carved BEEGAMUDRE HOUSE – using the original spelling of our family name. My grandfather dropped one of the e's.

My paternal grandmother, Bhagirathi, at the time of her marriage to Krishna in 1925, when she was fifteen.

Nagasha, a retired engineer, is seventy-two and looks nearly six feet tall. His wife is sixty and shorter than me. I'm struck by a resemblance between him and a picture of my grandfather Krishna taken when he retired.

In the living room is a carpet with contemporary versions of Indian symbols like wavy lines and pierced diamonds, a table with four cane chairs, and a glass cabinet full of handicrafts. Also two tables with inlaid scenes. The dining room is even more bare: no furniture, but the walls have framed pictures of gods and goddesses and some family photos. My uncle and aunt have five children and eight grandchildren. According to Appa, Nagasha and his wife spend a lot of money feeding priests at festival time.

Our dinner has many courses. Appa and Nagasha sit on the floor and eat with their right hands while my aunt serves us. She insists that I sit at a small table and eat with a spoon. Lemon rice, ladies' fingers (okra), a sweet drink meant to be the starter, rice with yogurt, pancakes made with coconut and brown sugar. I'm stuffed. Our conversation through the meal is mostly reminiscences of the family. After promising to visit again, we leave.

In the evening, Appa talks about places to see in India and about marriages in our family. He mentions Mom's uncle, the first native governor of Bombay. Another set of relations married into the Vepa family, one of the elite families of India. He says that when nephews and nieces lived with my grandfather, who paid to have all of them educated, he would draw with chalk the spaces they were allotted to sleep on the verandah floor. Also, I discover it was from Madras, not Calcutta as I'd thought, that my grandfather's brothers ran away to Burma. No matter. In my novel "Nomads" it will be Calcutta, since I have to go there to get my flight to Rangoon. Appa praises Rajini and Usha, the wives of Aunt Ratna's sons. Says she knows how to arrange marriages. Wonder if I should ask Ratna to find me a wife?

MOTHER OF THE WORLD

My maternal grandmother, Sonti Venkatlakshmi:
"Our Mother About September 1950."

THE SONTIS of the Madras Presidency were a distinguished family who produced the first Indian governor under the British. He was my mother's maternal uncle and his name was S. V. Ramamurthy, S for Sonti. He was the senior-most civil servant in Bombay when the governor died, and so my mother's uncle was made acting governor until a British replacement could "come out." Acting, perhaps, but still a governor and so, as my mother often said, "He was knighted by the viceroy himself." Everyone claimed they knew he was destined for greatness. It was said that, as a boy, he was so punctual – so exact – that neighbours could set their watches when he left for school.

Sonti Ramamurthy had sisters, three of them. There's a type of magic that skips generations so that children are more like their grandparents than like their own parents. This is why my mother used to say that I was especially like two of my cousins – two out of all my cousins on her side of our vastly extended family. Unlike the others, we supposedly cared more about people than about things. As to why we were so alike, it was because our grandmothers were the Sonti Sisters, and there's also magic in threes.

Unlike my Chintakindi grandfather, my Sonti grandmother – my *Ammamma* – seems more real than he does to me because my mother's stories about her were fond ones. All of them except for, understandably, the story of her death. As with Hanuman, I have both photographs and heirlooms. I keep his pocket watch out of sight but I keep my grandmother's *puja* ware (utensils for household religious ceremony) in plain sight. Like the watch, the *puja* ware is tarnished; unlike that silver watch, though – that half-hunter pocket watch – the *puja* ware is pewter.

Two of the pieces match. These stand four inches high and are for holding incense sticks. They taper in from their round bases, then up and out into cones with fluted mouths. The figures are in relief. On one holder are goddesses and, between them, symmetrical vines. A dancing goddess holds her left leg high with her knee bent. The other goddess also seems to be dancing, but she has no legs; from her narrow waist down, she's a snake. She's a *nagini* (a female snake goddess). On the second holder is a somewhat pastoral scene. A tiger, passing a leafy tree, chases a stag past a palm tree. The stag is headed for a thatched hut under another leafy tree. Turn the holder past this hut and once again the tiger chases the stag past the palm.

The other two pieces of *puja* ware, also four inches long, don't match. One lies flat with three petal-shaped depressions for holding oil. The second is a spoon for holy water. Its roundly perfect bowl widens into a lotus, then narrows into an etched column. On top of this column, at the end of the spoon, is a cobra. This is my favourite piece, not only for its weight but also for its perfection. The cobra balances the bowl, visually and physically. I can place the spoon on the edge of a ruler and watch the spoon tilt first towards the bowl, then towards the cobra. If I wait long enough, the spoon comes to rest with the bowl below the axis of the spoon at one end and, at the other end, above the axis, the cobra flaring its hood.

My Sonti grandmother's name was Venkatlakshmi. The Venkat would have been after our family god, Lord Venkateswara of Tirumala. The Lakshmi would have been for the goddess of fortune, the giver of wealth, also called Sri. She was the wife of Vishnu the Preserver. Each time he came to earth as an avatar, she came to earth as his wife. When he was Rama, the god-king hero of *Ramayana*, she became Sita, the queen who is abducted by the King of Lanka. Lakshmi is often shown with Vishnu on the great serpent Sesha, but when she's worshipped alone – in her own right – she's worshipped as the female energy of the Supreme Being, who is both female and male. Then she is called *Loka-mata*, mother of the world.

And Venkatlakshmi was the mother of my mother's world. My mother needed someone like her because my mother was the younger of fraternal twins, born in 1930, and she liked to think of herself as delicate. The twins' brothers were both older than the girls. The family's mother tongue was Telugu but the children attended secondary school in English, and Venkatlakshmi helped them with their lessons. She may not have been educated, but she became educated. Or so my mother said. As before, her sister recalls this quite differently. My aunt says Venkatlakshmi had been tutored some years earlier by members of the Canadian Baptist Mission. She says that my great grandmother was so orthodox that, even though Venkatlakshmi sat on one end of a mat and the missionary sat on the other end, after he left, Venkatlakshmi had to take what we call in India a head bath – to wash away his pollution.

This much is certain, though: Venkatlakshmi taught her children humanity, something Hanuman had mislaid among his formulae and theorems. At the same time, she managed a large household: servants, four children and – when he was home from his distant university – a husband.

The children studied in the light of kerosene lamps, and this was my mother's favourite story: how she came to study under electric lights. During the 1940s, the rich houses of Vizag-Waltair became electrified – not with cables running to houses from transformers but with individual household generators. Once, when Hanuman was home, Venkatlakshmi suggested that he have a generator installed and the house wired for electricity. He wouldn't hear of it. She couldn't appeal to his vanity by saying, "Other houses have them." It might not have worked, in any case, because he might have made unkind remarks about her more distinguished family. And so she waited until he left for the following school year. Then she did the most courageous thing of her life. She had a generator installed in the back of the house. The wiring would have spoiled the effect: twisted, brown wires were strung from column to column in the inner courtyard; panels of switches, controlling ceiling fans and lights, displaced paintings; sockets cluttered corners; unshaded light bulbs stuck out from the thick, whitewashed walls. But now, at last, the children studied under electric lights and in breezes from ceiling fans. She also ordered a wireless and had it installed in the main room. And yet, for all her cleverness, she lay awake at night dreading Hanuman's return. Perhaps she hoped he might never return.

He did. He noticed the lights and fans. He frowned at the sockets and wiring, and he flicked the switches. Following him from room to room, she waited for him to explode; to scold her for spending so much money without his permission; for waiting till he had gone away. Then he saw the wireless and turned it on. The static must have been loud, the air charged as if storm clouds were gathering. But the storm never came. Hanuman dashed outside and grabbed the first man he saw, a passing tinker. He pulled the man into the house and cried, "Look, the first wireless in this district! Isn't it grand?"

There were other stories, most of them about how Venkatlakshmi encouraged her children to study; to do well in college and then university. One was about my mother's insisting on writing exams though she had a fever, yet still earning a first class. This was something my father would hold against her later (her mania for studying), and I don't know whether she told him what she once told me: "It was my biggest mistake – marrying a man like my own father."

As for the photographs, I have five of Venkatlakshmi including two on the holy hill at Tirumala. The other three were posed in studios. In one, she sits with a sister. They're both middle-aged. They both look like mothers of the world. Venkatlakshmi has what used to be called a lazy eye; her right pupil faces the camera but her left pupil is in the outside corner of that eye. Since the photo isn't a close-up, the displaced pupil isn't noticeable. But it is noticeable in an enlargement marked in my mother's hand, "Our Mother, About September 1950." That is, it would be noticeable if someone hadn't drawn in Venkatlakshmi's left pupil to match her right. The things we do to make our families appear normal: forget; gloss over; exaggerate. But one day, in a photo someone might have looked at a dozen times over fifteen years, the flaws emerge. If nothing else, like stories, the flaws bring a person to life.

In the photo I associate most with my mother, Venkatlakshmi poses in front of a faded backdrop and stands barefoot on a flowered carpet. She's wearing her jewellery (much jewellery), including earrings on her pierced ears and two jewelled studs on her nose. It was taken about the time of her marriage, perhaps long before she had children, since she looks young and lithe. She poses with her right elbow resting on an ornate, metal plant stand complete with braid – beaten, not woven. There are no flowers on the stand.

I associate this photo with my mother because of one taken of her twenty years later, in a different studio by a different photographer, in 1951. By then the family had moved from Vizag-Waltair to my hometown of Bangalore, and my mother was graduating from Bangalore Central College. She wears an academic robe on which is pinned a gold medal. She clutches a scroll. She wears thick-soled sandals and at her feet are two prize books. She poses with her left elbow resting on the carved head of an elephant. Flowers spring from its upraised trunk. The stand is plain, not ornate. So is the carpet; so is the backdrop.

The photos are like reflections in two mirrors – two because I can't decide which photo is the original and which is the reflection. Two mirrors because the photo of my mother recalls her mother's place in the home while the photo of

My maternal grandmother, Sonti Venkatlakshmi, about the time of her marriage in the early 1920s.

Venkatlakshmi foreshadows her daughter's place in the world at large. For my mother would one day become an electrical engineer.

By the time of her gold medal graduation, the subcontinent had been partitioned into India and Pakistan. Hanuman was dead. Venkatlakshmi spent the final years of her life trying to claim her husband's providence fund from Punjab University in Lahore. There had been agreements, of course, that moneys would be repatriated for pensions and providence funds, but such things have a way of being forgotten when countries are split. In my mother's words, "It drove her mad." Venkatlakshmi swore out affidavits; she wrote letters; she waited on officials. Nothing worked. With all the problems India and Pakistan faced (resettlement, communal strife), who had time for the appeals of one widow? She came from a distinguished family, in any case. Why would she need her husband's providence fund? Why, indeed. She had no money of her own. She had four children in college and university. The money was hers by right. In the end, according to my mother, "She appealed to Pandit Nehru himself," and the prime minister intervened.

I didn't understand why she hadn't done this in the first place. How hard could it be to collect what was rightfully hers? I wouldn't understand until, years later, I found myself unable and unwilling to settle my mother's estate. Unable because I lived in Canada, the estate was in India, and certain men didn't want it settled. Unwilling because I wanted to avoid my grandmother's fate.

Mother of the world, and the world betrayed her. "It drove her mad," my mother said. Yes, it did. One day, sick at heart, weary from all the battles she had fought for her children, Venkatlakshmi poured kerosene on her sari and set herself on fire.

THE SECOND HOMEOPATH

Thursday, October 13, 1977

TODAY WE VISIT another doctor in Mysore, because Appa isn't impressed with the first. On the train, we talk to an elderly man who tells us many things about the countryside when he hears me ask Appa questions. The spiky, blue plants by the side of the tracks are called hedge plants in English. On the train, Appa gives a coin to a girl who comes down the aisle begging, but I shoo her away. Seems she's always on this train, accompanied by her father. She doesn't look needy; she has a schoolgirl's cloth bag on her shoulder. We have to take a bus to the new doctor's office. While waiting, we buy sugar cane juice spiced with ginger. The vendor grinds the sugar cane with a large cast iron gear mounted on a moveable concession stand.

The doctor, Shankar, shuffles into his office wearing a blanket as a shawl. He's unshaven and keeps wiping his face with a towel. His hands shake – from his influenza, I think. He puts no restrictions on my diet, gives me some sugar pills, and some ointment: a yellow paste containing coconut oil. His office is one corner of his verandah; on the wall are two diplomas, a chart of human bones, and a photo of his father. On a shelf are books and many test tubes. While he's with me, two sets of people come in: a mother with a cute boy wearing earrings, and a couple of women whose children are suffering from a reaction to smallpox vaccine. Soon I have my first attack of loneliness since having left Britain. Thanks to Dr. Powers, the therapist I saw in Ottawa for nine months, I've learned not to call it depression. It's either because of the skin problem or because the women made me realize how isolated I am out on Debur Road.

In the canteen of the medical college, Appa points out a framed, silver picture of a Swami. He's an ancestor of ours, Raghavendra Swami. He deserted his wife and child to become an ascetic and did miraculous cures. When it came time to die, he went into a trance and had his followers build the tomb over his body. Appa tells again the story, which I've heard many times, of how his father, Krishna, though not an orthodox Hindu, went to the swami's tomb after he cut himself shaving and the wound wouldn't stop bleeding. And was cured.

IF YOU PICK IT
IT WON'T HEAL!

Friday, October 14, 1977

I visit Dr. Shankar again in the morning. Appa and I hurry to catch the morning train. Being unshaven, I feel quite unclean. The doctor looks better today, having almost recovered from his influenza, but his hands still shake. He gives me a bottle of green oil to rub on after bathing. Later, with an hour to kill, I eat sweets at Bombay Tiffany's and look at inlaid coffee tables at the government emporium. The type I want,

My paternal grandmother, Bhagirathi, with Rakosh and Anand in Bangalore.

brown with inlaid white ivory chips in abstract borders and floral arrangements, cost anywhere from a modest 560 Rupees to 5,000 Rupees. There are also others things that I like, like the inlaid plaques with huge village scenes or jungles full of elephants.

After I return home, the watchman's wife tries to explain that there's a registered letter waiting for Appa at Debur. I don't understand, and she laughs. I can't stand that in foreigners. People would laugh in Austria (in 1975) when I didn't understand something on the menu. That evening, Appa and I ride our bicycles to Debur to see if the postmaster is at home. He isn't. We ride past the village, and on either side of the road are good views. To the left, south, nothing but rice paddies with the hills in the distance half-hidden by haze. To the right, north, is the main irrigation canal of the area. Hidden from view is the nearby river (the Kabini). On the way back, Appa talks about the joys of owning land.

Later it rains very hard and we have visitors: three labourers who sit on the verandah floor on mats; the primary school teacher from Debur – he and Appa talk the most; and an old gentleman, the secretary of a society in Debur. At first their presence annoys me; then I feel glad that people saw our light and found shelter. The rain lets up, then falls heavy again. All the while, I listen to the radio: mainly Tchaikovsky and Vitale.

More of My Mother's People

My grandfather Hanuman and my grandmother Venkatlak-shmi had four children: two boys and twin girls. The boys were named Joga-Rao and Amba-Rao, the girls Rama and Lakshmi.

Amba is usually a girl's name, while Rama is usually a boy's. In the epic *Mahabharata*, Amba is a princess who swears vengeance on the man who steals her from her bethrothed. So strong is her hatred that she becomes a man to seek revenge. In some versions, she returns as a man after her death; in others, she herself turns into a man. Rama we know as the seventh avatar of Lord Vishnu, the Preserver. In the epic *Ramayana*, Rama is the god-king of Ayodhya – a once and perfect king.

Lakshmi we know as the goddess of fortune, the giver of wealth, also called Sri.

None of my books tells me who Joga is.

1: Birthday Pictures

Besides the photograph from the holy hill of Tirumala – the one in which Hanuman walks ahead of Venkatlakshmi and away from their children – I have only two portraits of my mother with her brothers and sister. These photos, black and white, rest under a single white matte in a single wooden frame.

The first photo was taken in 1931. I know, because my mother told me it was taken on her first birthday. The second photo was taken in either 1948 or 1951. In 1948, the twins would have turned eighteen; in 1951, they would have come of age. Only a special occasion would have called for a studio portrait like this: the girls in their finery; the eldest boy in a suit; the second in his good college clothes.

Each photo by itself intrigued me as a boy. Side by side like this now, they fascinate me.

Like the portrait marked "Our Mother, About September 1950" – the one on which someone carefully drew her left pupil – the photo of Venkatlakshmi's children in 1931 has also been altered. Not retouched, as we would call it now, but touched up. The photographer himself likely did this. He darkened the *tilak* or bindi on the foreheads of the girls and the eldest boy; he darkened the eyes and eyebrows of each girl. It seems like such a typically Indian thing to do, especially to the girls' eyes. Yet nothing is drawn onto the later photo. Nothing needed to be drawn onto it. And there are other contrasts.

In the earlier photo, the boys are dressed alike; so are the girls. In the later photo, each of the four is dressed differently. This is only as it should be, for they're no longer children, they're individuals and adults. Finally, the second photo is clearer, more detailed, more full: a star design on the carpet; cut flowers in the brass pot on the stand; painted daisies climbing the painted column towards the painted fern. There's more than technology at work here; more than the simple fact that the first photo is an enlargement while the second was taken with a superior camera. Both physically and metaphorically, they move from casual to refined.

When I look at these portraits, I find myself thinking about my grandmother, Venkatlakshmi. I imagine her emotion while she looked from one to another, and I know that her emotion also changed. In 1931, she must have been proud. Seventeen or twenty years later, with her children grown up, she must have been more than proud. She must have been astonished.

2: *The Rocket Scientist*

MY UNCLE AMBA-RAO's claim to fame was this: like thousands of people, he helped the United States reach the moon. At Huntsville, Alabama, he was part of the team – he may even have led it – that tested the command module of the Apollo spacecraft for the stresses of take off and re-entry.

Amba-Rao was my favourite uncle on my mother's side. There's a picture, taken of me on my first birthday, in which I clutch a car, a gift from him. I remember it was red, had white tires, and was made in either Germany or England. Many of those early gifts, like a red and white teddy bear from my Aunt Rama, were made in Germany or England. I was the first child on my mother's side of the family, after all.

During the years I spent with my father in Ottawa and Kingston and in Bethlehem, Pennsylvania, we saw Amba-Rao often and he gave me more gifts: a dark green Parker ballpoint pen; even a stuffed baby alligator, its skin leathery, which he left on our dining table and waited patiently for me to touch. I liked him for his sense of humour, his gruffness, his almost childish desire to please children. But just as I didn't have to live with my grandfather Krishna or my Uncle Ananda, I didn't have to live with my Uncle Amba-Rao. During my youth, before diabetes started crippling him, and his hands started freezing into leathery claws, I used to think that he looked – and acted – like Spencer Tracy. It was through Amba-Rao that my parents met. He and my father had been – and always would be – the best of friends.

3: The Other Twin

WHILE GROWING UP, I associated my Aunt Rama with Bombay, perhaps because, until I saw it as an adult, I had always considered it exotic. And I've tended to associate her with exotic places because she and her husband, my Uncle Kochu, always seem to have lived in such places. He'd be-

My mother's people: Joga-Rao and Amba-Rao, with Lakshmi and Rama in Vizag in September 1951, when the twins turned twenty-one.

come an astronomer by accident. He'd wanted to be an historian but fell ill during his social science finals. By the time he had to write his science exams, he had recovered, and so he became an astronomer and not an historian.

Rama married some years after my mother did. By then my parents were separated. I think my father was best man at Rama and Kochu's wedding, though he had not known him before. My mother did not attend.

Unlike my mother, Rama always looked elegant in her sari, even in the West. She stayed with Kochu wherever he moved, which was not nearly as often as my father did. Besides states like Massachusetts, where Kochu spent time at Harvard, he and Rama lived in West Virginia and Hawaii, teaching and doing research at various universities. I never saw them in Hawaii, but I did see them in West Virginia. To me, coming from what was then called a broken home, they seemed a perfect family. They had two young children, a boy and a girl. We all went to Monticello, the home of Thomas Jefferson: statesman, inventor, author of the Declaration of Independence. An ideal place to visit.

Much later – even later than this India trip, when I missed them in Bombay – Rama and Kochu would move to Baltimore and then Vancouver. I would see them most often there, in their house on the edge of the UBC Endowment Lands: he in his study or in the living room listening to Bach; she in her garden, feeding tea leaves to her roses and making plans for the children. The boy was named Ravi Shankar Menon after the great Indian musician; the girl was named Kusum. Both of them would have their doctorates by their early twenties: Ravi his PhD, Kusum her MD. I would finish my twenties, then drift into my thirties, as a BA (Hon.).

One last thing about my Aunt Rama. She and my mother may not have been identical twins, but on the phone they sounded identical. Not in the way they spoke – Rama never plaintively like my mother – but in the pitch of the voice and the rhythms of their language. Even ten years after my mother's death, it would take me aback: answering the phone and hearing a voice – my mother's and yet not my mother's – saying, "Hello-how-are-you-both?" Then feeling grounded somehow, part of the past and yet free of it, at last. Or so I thought. Or so I hoped.

Dear *Playboy*

Saturday, October 15, 1977

IN THE MORNING, Appa goes to Chamarajanagar, south of Nanjangud, to see about having boxes that he had shipped from Vancouver delivered here. I write the outline for the first chapter of "Nomads" and again flee the wasps. Fall asleep under the mosquito net. Appa makes a late lunch.

This house belongs to an M. J. Sethu-Rao, a young advocate. He visits with a friend to check up on the watchman and it's the first time that the watchman and his wife and son work outside all day. They're repairing the irrigation and drainage ditches, whose banks had caved in from last night's rain.

I trap two huge black and red butterflies in a plastic jar while they sit on a bush outside the door. Kill them with kerosene and let them dry on Kleenex. One's in excellent condition; the other one isn't. I feel worse about throwing it away than I do at the sight of beggars. Or of naked children playing outside hovels beside railway tracks.

Sunday, October 16, 1977

NOT A VERY GOOD DAY. Mainly taken up with suffering from, and worrying about, my awful skin. Resort to using cortisone ointments on my face and hands.

Yesterday evening, seven boxes arrived. The men let the boxes drop to the floor from their shoulders and Appa yelled at one of them. Today, we unpack these boxes. They hold what little Appa didn't sell or give away when he left Vancouver. In one of the boxes is the set of Napoleon plates I'd bought for him in Paris back in '75. He's upset that the men broke two of these plates. Doesn't really bother me.

In the evening it rains and we have another visitor, a retired station master who lives in Mysore but has land nearby. Good music all evening on the shortwave.

Monday, October 17, 1977

SOMETHING OF A WASTED DAY. Appa comes with me to Dr. Shankar's office – he's my new homeopath. but leaves when it gets too late. About eleven, the doctor finally emerges from his bedroom. Gives me a bottle of red oil and tells me to apply it as often as necessary. Also says to bear up to a slight increase in aggravation. I don't leave till 11:45 because he takes his sweet time packing medicines for someone else. At the government emporium, I buy incense and sandalwood cones (to repel mosquitoes); meanwhile, I'm unable to get up my nerve to start a conversation with an American woman. From the city bus stand, I catch a bus to Appa's college. Have to ask half a dozen people, many whose English is poor, which bus to take. Jump on and push a man, who refuses to move out of the way, off his feet. Too bad, so sad.

NIE is still closed thanks to the students' strike and I'm unable to get any books from the institute library. Appa barely escapes having to do extra work for a Saraswati *puja* (a religious ceremony). We walk partway to the railway station in a downpour, flag a bus, then walk some more. My feet are wet and the back of my knees ache to be scratched, but I've made a pact with myself not to scratch. Dr. Shankar said that I should try to evoke the words of Vivekananda: "Strength! Strength!" On the train, Appa and I have to sit in different compartments. I watch a pretty girl in a sari talking and laughing with two friends. She holds a lesson plan from the Maharani Teachers' College. At night I ask him to tie my hands together so I won't scratch my face. After an hour or so, I free my hands. Scratch my arms and left leg badly.

Tuesday, October 18, 1977

IN THE MORNING, I bike to Debur to get a registered letter. We've been trying to get it from the postmaster for three days. His working hours are 9:30 to noon but he disappears around 10:30. I tell a child to find him and the postmaster finally appears. I explain that I've come for Appa's letter. The postmaster speaks little English but he repeats the word "rules." I prepare myself for an argument that doesn't materialize because he accepts the letter of authorization Appa prepared for me.

Bike back in an east wind that hurts my eyes, already aggravated by the glare and the tightness of my face. Twice, people come to the door. I don't understand one; the other needs to use a bicycle pump, which we don't have. In the afternoon I rub my face while trying to take a nap. Sethu-Rao, the young advocate, visits and we chat. He says land in this area costs 6,000 to 8,000 rupees, much less than what Appa had estimated. Sethu-Rao also says that his brother in Mysore can sign the library loan form I need to borrow books from the institute. I write a letter to Harry B.; we were both in the Governor General's Foot Guards when we studied at Carleton in Ottawa.

Around evening, there's a downpour. Locals find shelter in our verandah from the rain. There's an old woman who talks a lot, a young man, a grizzled man carrying a gunny sack, three other women, and three other men. I sit and watch while they all talk loudly and Appa prepares our dinner. Tonight's sunset is lovely: yellow-orange with the bottoms of purple clouds tinged with gold. The colour lasts a long time in the sky.

My dreams are becoming more interesting. Last night a woman visited me. She was dark and had large breasts barely concealed by her white top. Can't remember what we did. Sounds like a letter to the *Playboy* Advisor:

Dear Playboy,
You'll never believe what happened last night.

The only photo I've seen of my paternal grandfather, Krishna, and my grand-mother Bhagirathi with all of his natural children; taken in Hassan in the 1930s.

CHOCOLATE CAKE, GUAVA JAM

MY FIRST WINTER in Canada, my father had a friend called Mazumdar. He must have had a first name but we called him simply this. I liked repeating it, rolling that last syllable like (as I would learn) brandy on the tongue: Maz-um-dar. His wife's name was Erica. She was blond and beautiful and I fell in love with her chocolate cake. Fragrant with schnapps, heady for a boy of six rediscovering smells. Even in school, where teachers used Gestetners, where we coveted handouts fresh from the press, inhaled the alcoholic vapour of the purple type. Much later, I would wonder about Erica's secret, illicit ingredient. Was it that heavy Sicilian wine called Marsala or that gin called Holland's?

When the Mazumdars moved, I tempered my regret by chanting their name. "Never make fun of names, my father said. "And always spell them correctly. It shows respect."

Thus, I became conscientious about names; wondered why strangers felt no such compulsion with ours. In fact, my saying Begamudre left them speechless. Some mistook it as a lapse into a foreign tongue. Which it was, in a way. Others found it hard to pronounce, let alone spell. To head off, "Pardon?" and my own annoyance, I immediately spelled our name.

My first winter back in India, 1977–78, was a summery one. Canadian smells of wood smoke, of damp wool gave way to sandalwood incense, bare skin. My father was taking a tonic for high blood pressure. The tonic smelled like cherry brandy but more tropical, like guava jam. Once, I cycled into town for his refill, the bottle wrapped, its neck sticky with crystallized syrup. Prescriptions here were not called this: not filled or refilled. They were compounds. Compounded. By a compounder.

"Who is this for, please?" the compounder asked. Dribbles of tonic, sweetly hardened on the label, had obscured the name. "Mr. Begamudre," I said. "B-e-g-a-"

He interrupted with, "Sir!" This one syllable, this rolling *sirrh* begged an end to condescension. "Sir," he said. "I know how to spell."

A calendar picture of Lord Venkateswara of Tirumala.

THE SKELETONS OF DEBUR ROAD

An Unfinished Story

MY GOOD FRIEND Shankar took a towel from his medical bag. Ignoring our raised eyebrows, he unwrapped a bottle of whiskey. Then he asked the peon to bring him a large glass. The man stood with his head bowed as though it pained him to contradict a guest – as opposed to contradicting a member, which he did as often as he judged safe. "I do not know where the good doctor is from," the peon said. "We have prohibition in Madras."

"I know that," Shankar said kindly, "but Dr. Devraj is on the club committee and he is saying nothing." He handed the peon a five-rupee note that the man tucked out of sight after I nodded to him. I betrayed no dismay over Shankar's bottle, not because I approved but because I hoped it might loosen his tongue. He had been less than talkative during the proceedings of our conference. Now, ever the bully among us, K rubbed his hands with a satisfaction bordering on delight. "I thought so," he exclaimed. "Shankar, you are exhibiting symptoms of liver cirrhosis. You are also constantly smoking that wretched pipe. Is this any way for a doctor to treat his own body?"

Shankar waited for his glass, which he proceeded to fill.

"That is where we Indians have failed in adopting western medicine," he told us. "Most westerners do not understand that to treat the body one must first treat the mind. Besides, gentlemen – and I mean you, too, K – I have not been a practising doctor since I left Nanjangud."

K smirked off the insult while offering me a Dunhill gold-tip. He lit mine with his silver lighter before lighting one for himself. Then he observed, "I had no idea that town doctors made so much money that they could retire to Bangalore at forty!"

"I did not retire," Shankar said. He smacked his lips after taking a rather large sip of his whiskey and looked appreciative even if it was IMFL – Indian-made Foreign Liquor. "There is no prohibition in Bangalore, thank God! I thought you knew, K. I quit my practice." He slowly lit his pipe. All of us, K included, watched the ceiling fan disperse the Turkish smoke over the billiard and card tables elsewhere in the room. The smoke combined with the smell of leather chairs to enhance an already masculine atmosphere. We had recently admitted our first female members but, for reasons known only to them, they avoided our games room.

I suspected we all wished to ask the same question: why had Shankar quit his practice? No one asked it. Instead we sipped our coffee (except K, who affects North Indian habits and thus prefers tea) while we waited for Shankar to continue. When he finally did, careful as always to include all of us in his monologue, he spoke at length. None of us found the courage to ask him the point of his narrative. We merely hoped – in vain, it appeared – that he would finally explain his desertion of our ranks.

Few of us know what it is like to be a town doctor, Shankar began, although my friend Devraj here seemed to think that T. Narasipur was a fine place to practise until this college lured him to Madras. There are certain advantages, like the peace and quiet of sitting on the verandah and listening to the wind in the coconut palms, or the quaintness of telling time by the whistles of trains instead of by the roaring of motorcars and lorries. And, of course, there is the advantage of working in a small dispensary with only a nurse and a compounder – some of whom are such jokers that one would think they were created by Hanuman himself instead of by God. I had just such a compounder in Nanjangud. One night, after locking my dispensary and taking my evening meal, I had settled down to my daily reading of the *Bhagavad Gita* when Dunu, my compounder, knocked on the verandah door. "Do not tell me," I said. "You want to borrow my cycle so you can warn some unfortunate person that the mixture you dispensed today will cure head cold instead of malaria."

"Why do you laugh at me sir?" he asked He grinned while wiping his feet on the coir mat in the doorway. "I gave the wrong mixture once only, once in a million times!"

"And it nearly cost me my licence," I reminded him. "What is it? You will wake my wife with all this noise."

"I have news, Doctor. Such news! I was walking near the toddy shop on Bus Stand Road when I overheard the most amazing tale!"

"Another of your amazing tales?" Sighing, I waved him into the verandah. After he settled on the floor, I asked, "Well, what has happened tonight? A hero from *Mahabharata* has come to life?"

"No, sir. I was walking near the toddy shop on Bus Stand Road when I overheard a taxi driver from Mysore. I do not concern myself with other people's business but this fellow was talking so loudly a stone deaf man could hear. Some fellow paid him sixty rupees to drive him all the way from

Mysore Railway Station to Debur. Sixty rupees for twenty-odd miles only."

"No wonder the driver was drunk," I said "He made thirty rupees' profit at least."

But Dunu leapt to the man's defence. "Where is the profit? He has to drive all the way back to Mysore in the dark now and without a passenger. Who will hire him at this time of night? Besides, he said sixty rupees and the bandaged fellow agreed."

"What bandaged fellow?"

"Why, the bandaged fellow who hired the driver!" Dunu clucked his tongue in annoyance at my apparent inability to decipher what, to him, was manifest. "The fellow who got down at Debur had his head completely wrapped in bandages!"

"So what?" I asked.

"Abbah!" Dunu shrieked. "I tell a doctor a bandaged fellow has arrived in our district and he says, 'So what?' The poor fellow might be in pain. He might be near death!" By this time Dunu actually had leapt to his feet and was waving his arms like a madcap railway signalman.

"Have you been drinking as well?" I asked sharply.

"One sip only. I gave the driver a *beedi* and he gave me a sip from his toddy. Where is the harm in that? A smoke for a sip."

Exasperated, I said, 'Get out, madcap, before I begin searching for another compounder!"

"I am going," he said, although he made no move towards the door. "But if I go, you will not learn who this fellow is until tomorrow morning, and you will not hear of this from such a reliable witness as me."

"Why should I care who the fellow is?" I demanded.

Dunu rolled his eyes up at the ceiling. "He is a doctor and he says he does not care? Doctor, this fellow is none other than the son of Lalita, Mr. Krishnamurthy's eldest daughter, who married the professor from Ootacamund and left with him for America."

Incredulous at such wealth of detail from a taxicab driver, I demanded, "The driver knew all this?"

"Of course not, Doctor sir! How can he know everyone from our area if he is from Mysore? He asked the fellow what business he had at Debur, and the fellow said he had come back from America to settle in his native place. How many people from this area have gone away to America besides yourself and then come back?"

Dunu had a point there and yet, beyond establishing the identity of the bandaged man, he had told me little. He waited for me to offer coffee in return for his news. When I did not, he bade me many sincere wishes for a restful night.

I could not take up my book after he left. Instead, I lit my pipe and watched with satisfaction while mosquitoes fled the smoke.

When I was a boy, Mr. Krishnamurthy's daughter Lalita was famous in Nanjangud for her delicate condition. Her nerves, it was said, prevented her from doing much beyond helping her mother at home and so Lalita had never attended our school. Thus, long after she had married and left India, her name had been remembered in our district by those who cared to do so. I considered paying her son a visit but soon dismissed the idea. After all, he had returned not to the town of his birth but to a village some furlongs distant. This meant he wished no visitors. As much as I longed to ask him many questions about progress in America, I decided to leave him alone unless he should call on me for help with his injuries. Within a week, however, I changed my mind. I resolved to meet this foreign-returned prodigal son because of the new tales with which Dunu entertained me.

At first, there was little substance to these tales because Lalita's son did nothing. He lived in the house he had rented from the district's most wealthy *zamindar* (a landowner), Mr. Kempe Gowda, and was never seen outside. The only person allowed into his presence was Mrs. Kempe Gowda, who took him three meals a day cooked in her house. Then, on the fourth day, the tales piqued my curiosity.

"Strange goings-on at Debur last night, sir," Dunu said. "One of the *zamindar's* watchmen was attacked by a skeleton! He ran away and the skeleton stole a cart full of sugar cane. It is true. I heard of it from the watchman's brother himself." Then, the next day: "Even stranger goings-on last night, sir. The ghost of a Muslim frightened the cows belonging to the Debur postman. One of them dropped dead in its tracks!"

When I asked how people knew it had been the ghost of a Muslim, Dunu snorted triumphantly. "Do we Hindus bury our dead so they rot to the bones? Besides, only a Muslim ghost would frighten such a devout Hindu's cows!" And the next day: "Extremely strange goings-on, sir. A skeleton flew over Debur last night. It chased the postman into the upper canal and his son into the lower canal and the schoolteacher into the Kabini itself!" When I asked how one skeleton had managed to chase three men in three different directions, Dunu threw up his hands. "God has three faces, sir! Why can a skeleton not have three skulls?"

"Because this apparition was a Muslim," I reminded him. "As far as we know, Allah has only one face." At this, Dunu shut up. As much as he wanted to borrow my cycle to investigate the mysteries further – during dispensary hours, of course – I claimed this prerogative for myself. I intended to speak only with Lalita's hermit son and not with the villagers, for I knew that even a foreign-returned man has not the power to fly; that the source of the mystery could be only in the villagers' childish imaginations. Accordingly, after we locked the dispensary at noon on Saturday, I changed out of my doctoring shirt and trousers and hurried through my midday meal. Then, tying up the ends of my dhoti and donning an old soft cap, I cycled west from Nanjangud towards Debur. The Ganesh Rice Mill sounded fairly quiet but, across the road, men cut swaths in the sugar cane field. It promised to be a good harvest and soon we would celebrate Sankranti. As you know, this involves driving cows over fire to separate those that will be bred from those that will not because, if they balk at the flames, they may balk at the bull's horn. One does not see such time-honoured techniques of animal husbandry by practising in a city. I rather doubted anyone would allow the Debur postman's herd near the fire, however, since it had been cursed by a ghost. A Muslim ghost, at that.

Ten minutes' cycling brought me to the only house on Debur Road: the house of Mr. Kempe Gowda the *zamindar*, who greeted me warmly. With the income from three crops a year, he had managed to send all of his sons and daughters to college. Still and all, he was not above grinding lengths of sugar cane for those he regarded as his equals. He brought me a tumbler of fresh cane juice with a sprinkling of lime and I remarked on his generosity. When I yielded to temptation and finally asked about the villagers' tales, he became his usual heated self.

"Such people talk, not people like us," he said. "We all know it is fashionable for ghosts to steal crops during harvest. That is why village people are too tired to work properly during the day!" When I turned him from his thrice-yearly complaint and asked about Lalita's son, he became expansive. "Ah, Mr. Srinivas does not disturb me and I do not disturb him. Some months ago I received a letter from him saying he wanted to rent a house from me. 'Of course,' I wrote back. 'Stay in our very house, if you wish. Nothing is too good for the son of Lalita, who went to Canada...'"

"I thought the family moved to America?" I mused aloud.

"Abbah! You are again listening to the talk of uneducated fellows! They went to Canada. I can show you Mr. Srinivas's aerogramme if you wish to confirm its origin." I assured him this would not be necessary. "Upon receiving his second letter, in which he insisted upon having separate quarters, I politely asked one of my tenants to vacate my Debur house and kept everything in readiness for Mr. Srinivas's arrival. He is a model tenant. It is the toddy only that causes all these tales. How is it these people come to work for me when and if they please and still have money to go into Nanjangud to watch films? Or to visit the toddy shop on Bus Stand Road?"

I hmm'd noncommittally and handed back my empty tumbler. "Have you seen Mr. Srinivas since his arrival?" I asked. "How serious are his injuries?"

"What does an ignorant *zamindar* know about medical matters? Ask me about land. I know everything about owning land. I spoke with him once only, in the late evening, and he kept the light off in the house. He said it hurts his eyes. Even my good wife does not see him when she brings him his food. He remains in the darkest corner. Perhaps he will let you examine him. I can give you a letter of reference, if you wish."

I declined his generous offer and prepared to remount my cycle.

"One moment!" Mr. Kempe Gowda cried. He dashed into his house and emerged with a papaya and a lime. "You will please take these to Mr. Srinivas. He will be wanting a snack soon, but he does not allow my wife to take him anything because she will disturb his afternoon sleep. He very much likes fresh fruit, especially limes."

I thanked my host and tucked the papaya under one arm. The lime I tucked under my cap, then set off. On the way to Debur, I passed two young goatherds cursing one another's mothers to pass the time and was myself passed – by the westbound H.D. Kote bus. As usual, it carried too many passengers and too much luggage for anyone's safety. Now the goatherds laughed when I began coughing in the cloud of dust raised by the bus. I decided not to scold them in case they began cursing my mother, as well. Ordinarily, I would have asked the Debur postman where to find Mr. Srinivas's abode but, as he was one of the villagers bearing a grudge against the new resident, I went in search of the house myself. It proved easy to find for, in that March heat, only one dwelling in the village had its front door shut. The bungalow Mr. Kempe Gowda had generously rented to Mr. Srinivas at such short notice turned out to be a hut like so many others in Debur. It was roofed not with fine Mangalore tiles like the larger houses in the village but rather with local, burnt-clay tiles. Directly I knocked on the door, I heard a voice demand in what sounded like a genuine American accent, "Who's there?"

"J.W. Shankar," I called, ignoring the small crowd of children gathering around my cycle.

"What do you want?"

"Only to speak with you. I heard you have injuries and thought–"

"Go away," he said.

Seeking to placate him, I replied, "Very well. But you had best take this fresh fruit I am leaving on your doorstep before the children take it instead."

"Leave it inside the door then," he commanded.

I opened the door cautiously and waited for my eyes to adjust to the lack of light in the house. All the shutters were closed. I could barely discern the figure huddled on the dusty floor in the far corner of the main room. It was the only room in the house.

"Just leave the stuff," he said.

I did so but, as I pulled back, he said, "Wait. You're the doctor from Nanjangud, aren't you? Mrs. Kempe Gowda thinks she has to fill me in on everything that's happened in the twenty years I've been in Canada. She said you've been to the States."

Resisting the urge to enter any farther, I told him that, yes, I had studied at Johns Hopkins after receiving my MB BS. "But that was over fifteen years ago," I added.

"It's still nice to hear someone speak good English for a change." He sighed. "Would you like to come in? I'm sorry if I was rude."

My years in college and abroad had not erased my native cunning and so I pretended to think for much longer than it took me to hit upon a plan. If I made him wait until we conversed in a more leisurely manner, he might be more willing to tell me why he had returned from abroad. "I would very much like to visit but I am doing my rounds," I said. "Perhaps I could come back tomorrow?"

"Yes," he said eagerly. "Any time. Well, later in the evening is best. After supper."

"Of course." Using what little of my American vernacular I could recall, I said, "I shall see you."

The following evening, I set off for Debur again. This time, however, I went well provisioned. Before leaving Nanjangud, I bought *idlis* and curry at the hotel, filled a thermos bottle with sugar-cane juice purchased from a vendor, and hung a bunch of the small Nanjangud bananas over the centre bar of my cycle. Armed with all of this and my cycle lantern, I set off.

Mrs. Kempe Gowda had just left Mr. Srinivas's evening

meal at the door when I arrived at his house.

"You have come to examine our foreign-returned guest?" she asked.

"No," I replied, dismounting. "To talk only. He seems to be in no pain."

She massaged her left forearm, which was so thick that her bangles could not move enough to clink against one another. "But my pain is returning, Doctor."

"It is all the rich food you eat," I said and dared for once to laugh. "I keep telling you to cut out sweets and to drink milk. Why do you give milk to your husband and your children's sons only? Women also need calcium for their bones and teeth." When she frowned at a passing bullock cart, I appreciated she did not want advice, so I gave in. "Send someone to the dispensary Monday and I will have Dunu compound a mixture."

She smiled at me then, showing what few teeth remained in her head.

"Oh, thank you Doctor!" she said and waddled off. I believe that delivering Mr. Srinivas's three meals a day, which entailed a walk of two miles in total, was her only physical exercise.

Directly I knocked on the door, our hermit opened it. He turned away with his food into the farthest corner. "Thought that was you," he said. "Come on in. Might as well bring the bike in, too, or you might end up having to walk home in the dark."

I did as he advised, then removed from the handlebar the cloth bag containing the thermos and hotel food. "Would you like to eat these snacks, instead?" I asked.

He stopped in the midst of opening the tiffin carrier (a several-tiered lunch box) that Mrs. Kempe Gowda had delivered. "Sure," he said. "You get tired of cold leftovers pretty quick." He placed the tiffin carrier on the floor and leaned back into the protective gloom of his corner.

While I placed my cloth bag on the floor and picked up the tiffin carrier, I saw what little he must have hoped I would see. Srinivas's face was completely wrapped in white bandages from his hairline down to his throat. These bandages left only his ears, nose and lips visible. The curious flatness of his face surprised me despite the trimness of his body, which lacked even the slight bulge I associated with all men past twenty. After noting this little, I hurried back to the door and sat down with my back against it. We ate in silence – I the cold rice and *sambar* from the round tins of the tiffin carrier; Srinivas the *idlis* and curry from the leaves in which the hotel had wrapped them with brown twine. Around him on the floor, books lay scattered on the ashes of sandalwood cones burned to keep away mosquitoes. In the corner to the left of me lay two suitcases open to display a variety of light, western clothing. But for the books and suitcases and an expensive portable radio plugged into the wall near him, little in the house was his own. Near the back door stood two battered buckets and an immersion coil for heating his bath water. I could see no taps or a toilet, so I supposed he drew water from the village well and relieved himself in the fields.

"You could not have asked for a more primitive existence," I said at last. "If you had come three years ago, there would not even have been electricity in Debur."

He shrugged. "Suits me just fine. Only problem is, I have to get the water at night. Should be a bit left, though."

I rose and, keeping my distance from him, poured some water from a brass pot to wash my hand. Then, while wiping my hand on my dhoti, I returned to my place by the door and watched him wash both of his hands. Clearly, he cared nothing for our custom of using only the right hand to eat. He wiped his hands on a towel and retreated to his corner.

VEN BEGAMUDRÉ

"You don't mind if we keep the light off, do you?" he
asked.

"Does it hurt the eyes?" I chanced.

He laughed drily as though wondering where I had heard
this news. "Something like that."

Neither of us spoke for a very long time. From a house
nearby I heard a couple arguing about their daughter's im-
pending marriage. Their voices were soon drowned out by
the closer wailing of a child. It could not be convinced that
milk could only be obtained in the morning. Finally I lit my
pipe and asked, "How is your mother? She is still remembered fondly in Nanjangud. Why, my mother said that people
would come from miles around to see the delicate tracery
that the sun left on her exposed skin."

Without any emotion, he replied, "She's dead."

"I am sorry," I told him. I said this with feeling although I
had said exactly this so many times during my practice to
mothers who lost their children in infancy or to grieving
women who, upon the deaths of their husbands, lost su-
premacy in their households to their daughters-in-law. "That
must have been a terrible shock. She could not have been
very old?"

"No," he said quietly, but not in reply to the latter question. "It wasn't a shock at all." Then, "You'd love to know why
I came back, wouldn't you?"

I said nothing. His manner of speaking had brought
back memories of conversations I had long ago had in
Maryland. Everyone in America loves: they love to read,
love to dance. Or they are always dying: dying for a cigarette, dying for a drink. I supposed the same held true for
everyone in Canada. I fancied that the whole of North
American existence could be summed up in the two expres-
sions I had so often heard: loving and dying. In this way,

178

Americans and Canadians are no different from anyone else in the world.

"Well," he said, mistaking my silence for embarrassment. "You can pretend you don't if you want to, but I've barely talked to anyone in the last week, so why don't we make a deal? I'll tell you what you want to know providing you don't cross-examine me."

I agreed to his request, made all the more intriguing by the criminal court terminology.

He pulled his knees up to his chest and sat staring at the ground for a long time as if deciding where to begin his autobiography. He took a sip of sugar cane juice and cleared his throat. Then, addressing the shuttered window, he began his tale.

"Two nights before my mother finally left us, I dreamt that she had died. I also dreamt that I had cried. Alone. And how had she died? I forgot this in the act of waking, an act that induces amnesia much as the shock of birth apparently does – those unwilling passages from darkness to light that erase everything we knew in the womb and much else we learn in sleep.

"'It is good to dream such things,' she said after I told her about her death. Not about my tears. 'It will make you strong.'"

I was nine going on ten. I had no idea why I should be strong...

THE REST OF THE CURE

October 19, 1977 to Year's End

AT LAST I TAKE UP my pen to fill the void of the last two
months. I left off because of the increasing discomfort caused
by my cure. The second day after my last entry was one of
the worst; yet the challenges that I face have only just begun.

All day my face burned, and I felt as though the skin had
tightened into a mask that wouldn't let me smile. That night,
I cried openly while Appa tried to comfort me. The next day,
the skin broke and began peeling off. While hastening the
peeling process, I rubbed my face and neck with a towel. The
results were disastrous. The skin oozed wetly. By morning
my face was frozen into a rigid mask. I could open my mouth
just enough to eat with a spoon as long as it held little food.
I endured this for at least two days and sank from despair to
despondency. Then, aided by a yellow ointment from Dr.
Shankar and more sugary pills, the outer layer of the skin
cracked and began to peel off. The dead skin was so rigid that
it curled down as it let go. Again and again, over many days,
I peeled it off and it re-grew, softer each time till finally the
flaking stopped. Yet had I known what I still had to endure,
I would have stopped the cure right then.

The next phase was so drawn out that I lost track of the

duration or exact sequence of events. My arms and hands, my legs and feet, my forehead, ears, and neck erupted in boils – but not all at the same time. The boils contained pus that, according to Dr. Shankar, was the poison in my system that was causing my chronic problems with dry skin. Since my face had first reacted to Dr. Shankar's internal medicine, I had stopped wearing my glasses from time to time. Now I left them off completely. I couldn't bear to look at the sickly white boils that covered my body or at the red, open wounds on my right foot.

I don't know how Appa could bear the sight. What would I have done without him? He bathed me twice a day and applied the ointment. When my feet and knees were so covered with boils that they wouldn't flex, he carried me into the bathroom or to the cab that drove us to Mysore. He endured my complaining and tolerated my tears when I awoke after having barely slept the night – thanks to the pain – only to find I was no better.

Worse than the pain was the anguish. After breakfast I would lie in bed doing nothing or perhaps reading a little – unable to write a word either in my journals or of my novel "Nomads." By mid-morning, the pain would come in my legs. I had to prop a pillow under my knees to find a comfortable position in which to lie. The pain would come again in the late afternoon. No wonder my nights were sleepless: I lay in bed all day; each time I turned at night, I had to awake enough to place my limbs and head in exactly the right position. As for the anguish, it made my five days at Stanford University Medical Centre (in June of 1975, after reacting to a vaccination that I should not have gotten) seem hardly serious. I don't remember ever despairing then because I knew that I was in excellent hands: in isolation and served by kindly nurses. Here, though, I was at the mercy of an alien system of medicine and, too frequently, I was alone. Sometimes I was convinced that I would go through life deformed by the bumps on my skin. They never seemed to subside or, if they did, they reappeared because I couldn't resist rubbing or scratching areas that had begun to heal.

Appa later admitted to me that one night I was in such low spirits, he wondered whether I would bother waking up the next morning. He was afraid that my body, with its resistance gone along with my willpower, would simply give up the fight.

Unable to read or write, I fantasized. The starting point was, of all things, winning the Seal Books First Novel Award for an immigrant novel that I was also writing. Around this single incident, I wove a new life for myself and played and replayed the scenes for myself. *I move to Montreal to begin researching the rest of "Nomads"; buy a sportscar – at first a Corvette, then a Jaguar E-Type; move to Vancouver via Philadelphia, St. Louis, Wichita, and Regina in order to visit friends and relatives; search for an apartment and furnish it; meet, fall in love with and marry a Swiss nurse; buy a house on the north shore of English Bay; raise a son and a daughter; and, finally, listen to them crying at my deathbed while my wife plays Chopin's* Second Piano Concerto. *My last request.*

At last the bumps began to subside and my spirits rose. There were relapses as new boils appeared, because my body apparently hadn't developed a complete immunity, but the day came when the scratching didn't cause new eruptions. Here I entered a difficult phase: I simply couldn't control the scratching. A combination of the natural healing process of the skin and its dryness in other areas made me scratch with no control. Days that I had to endure without medicine became unbearable. I resorted to tying myself to my bed in an effort to survive until Appa brought more ointment from Dr.

Shankar. One day was particularly bad and I cried aloud unashamedly – for the first time – cursing Appa for having no wife to be my mother. The boils had lasted perhaps three weeks, and this latest phase lasted perhaps two. At least I could read again, although still without my glasses. Towards the end I started making notes for "Nomads" and started plotting its scenes in my mind.

-→⁂←-

It's now December 30th, and I'm in the second phase after this hideous reaction to Dr. Shankar's medicine. This phase also has its worries because I've gone back to scratching the way I did before this cure started, i.e., scratching my whole body once a day and, even worse, my face. Appa has labelled the dark area on my forehead and around my eyes the Mask of Zorro. I know it bothers him that the scratching has returned. At the time of this writing, I feel better and am scratching less.

Dr. Shankar has given me a liquid with a coconut oil base to be applied before my bath – which I can now give myself twice a day – to be followed by the ointment. The two together bring much relief. He says that the physical part of the cure is over, but the mental part is not. The rest is up to me. I must not scratch and yet, when the itching starts, I respond automatically. If only for Appa's sake, I have to exert even more willpower than I have.

A word about the doctor. During the painful part of the cure, I had confidence in him; but, during the past month, my opinion of him has become very low. He may be a good doctor, but he keeps his patients waiting far too long. Also, as the morning wears on, he makes more frequent trips to his liquor cabinet and becomes garrulous and repetitive. Twice, he was actually staggering across the room by the time we left his house. How many times have I heard phrases like these (offered to me or, more importantly, to Appa because he was paying the bills): "He must take complete bath from head to foot. Complete bath with Lifeboy soap and wash the soap content thoroughly. Not to worry! He is very much improved. In another two weeks he will be very much relieved. In another two weeks he will be completely cured. I guarantee it. By the grace of God, I will see him through!"

One morning, when he was especially drunk, he told us a story that I suppose he thought would excuse his drinking and earn our sympathy. This it did. His wife, he said, was nursing the baby boy at her breast. He plucked at his own left breast and threw something invisible away. "One moment the baby was alive. The next moment it was no more." And, the more he drank, the less he thought of his own powers of healing and the more he thought of God's: "By the grace of God, I will see him through!"

To Appa, again: "You need not worry. I have studied his case thoroughly and I am confident that he is under my control. Only, he must take complete bath from head to foot. Complete bath with Lifebuoy soap and..."

I forgot to mention one other thing: During the days I thought that I might have to go through life disfigured and hideous, my thoughts turned to death. Perhaps this is only natural in a personality as serious as mine. *I heat a bucket of water in which to plunge my arms after slashing my wrists. The blood mingles with the water while I slip into oblivion. Appa finds me seated on the floor against the wall, dead and at peace.* Why I didn't do it, assuming my desire to die was genuine, I don't know. Perhaps it was because of the rosy future I had imagined for myself, or perhaps it was because I have a built-in mechanism that demands survival against any odds. Only God – certainly not our beloved Dr. Shankar – knows how I survived.

Prahlad's House

February 26, 1978

I'M FEELING CONSIDERABLY BETTER, so Appa and I go for a bicycle ride and stop at the house west of ours on the road from Nanjangud to Debur. It's the only other proper house on this road. It belongs to a farmer named Prahlad, a friend of our landlord, Sethu-Rao, the young advocate. I'd met him a few months earlier, when the two men stopped for a visit at our house. Prahlad is quite young and, like Sethu-Rao, he treats my father with respect and, I suppose, he thinks I'm special because I left India fifteen years ago to become a Canadian.

The exterior of his house and its supporting walls are built of brick covered with plaster. The roof slopes up from an A-frame supported by six-by-six-inch beams. Slanting to a point are two-by-fours, across which are nailed slats. The gaps between the slats are covered with flat, red-orange Mangalore tiles. One layer is enough to keep out rainwater, he tells us – Appa and me – and there's no place for scorpions to hide.

Prahlad gives us a tour of his house, which he lives in with his mother. The front and back doors are low and made of slabs of wood. There's a front verandah opening to the north that's enclosed by a diamond-patterned, large-holed wire mesh. The inside walls are decorated with religious motifs, a two-headed Mysore eagle, and photos of Prahlad's parents. The bathroom is large and contains a wood-fired stove under a large, copper kettle for heating water. The floors in the house are paved with stone slabs, about one yard square, from a place called Cuddapah. Sacks of grain line a wall of the main room, which contains one cot just inside the front door. The only other furnishings are some folding metal chairs and some tables, on which are two radios and a cassette recorder. Electricity is fed into the house by open wires and sockets. These are nailed onto the beams or set into the plaster with little effort to conceal them. Still, I suppose that after a while a person would get used to the sight.

Since I'm not considered an orthodox Hindu, I can't enter the kitchen, which is the preserve of Prahlad's mother. She is old and shakes. Drinking-water comes from a well behind the house, and here there's also a cowshed whose walls are woven from dry coconut palm fronds. The flush toilet is in an outhouse on the far side of an electric transformer that he points out to us.

Prahlad owns a pair of bullocks for every five acres of his land. *Jawar* (sorghum) is sown in April and reaped in June. In August, following heavy rains, rice is sown. After the rice is harvested, the straw is heaped and fed to livestock. There are four permanent workers on the land and Prahlad hires extra labour when he needs to. He does quite well.

The Demon King's Son

A Telling Retelling

THERE WAS ONCE A KING named Hiranyakasipu, whose name meant "golden robes". He lived in a city that moved. It could burrow through the earth or sail through the air. Most of the time, though, the city remained where it had been built: under the sea. It was no ordinary city, and Hiranyakasipu was no ordinary king. He was a demon.

The demons, who were bad, had once lived in heaven with the gods but the gods grew tired of sharing heaven and so they drove the demons out. Some, like Hiranya-Kasipu, built wonderful things like cities that moved. This pleased the gods, who gave such demons boons.

The king wanted to live forever and so he asked for a very great boon. Yet he did not say, "Let me live forever." He liked the sound of his own voice and so he said:

Let me not be killed by a man or a beast or a god;
During day or night;
Either inside or outside my house.

It sounded like such a wonderful boon, the gods could not refuse.

Before long, Hiranya-Kasipu forbade his subjects to worship the gods. The penalty for worshipping anyone but him was death. Each morning he asked his subjects, "How much do you adore me?" Each morning they said:

> We adore you as the sun and the moon and the stars;
> As the earth and the life-giving sea;
> As a father and as a god.

On holy days, to celebrate his power, he made the city move. It burrowed down through the seabed into the earth until the earth quaked. The city rose up through the sea until waves towered over the mountains. It sailed through the air until clouds quivered. The king stood on the balcony of his palace and said:

> I am the lord of the three worlds;
> The lord of heaven and earth and hell;
> The great Hiranya-Kasipu.

At the sound of his voice, the mountains shuddered and the air shivered. The clouds rained tears on the sea.

The gods began to worry. They went to the great Lord Vishnu – he of the blue skin and four arms, he of the peaceful gaze – and they asked him, "What shall we do?"

"Leave this demon king to me," Vishnu said. He watched and waited. He waited and watched.

Only one thing pleased Hiranyakasipu more than the sound of his own voice. This was his son, Prahlad, who lived with his teacher in the forest.

Here Prahlad learned what every future king must know. He learned the arts and sciences and scriptures. He also learned what every future king must never forget: to be hum-

ble. He did not learn this from his teacher. He learned it by
worshipping Vishnu. When Prahlad fixed his thoughts on
Vishnu, the lord filled Prahlad with joy.

One morning, the teacher took Prahlad to the city. The
king stood on his balcony. "How much do you adore me?" he
called. His subjects said:

We adore you as the sun and the moon and the stars;
As the earth and the life-giving sea;
As a father and as a god.

Prahlad frowned. He asked his teacher, "Have the people
never heard of Vishnu and the other gods?"

"Do not ask such questions," the teacher warned. He led
Prahlad into the palace.

Hiranya-Kasipu sat on his throne now. Nearby stood his
guards. He looked delighted to see his son. "And you?" the
king asked Prahlad. "How much do you adore me?" To this
Prahlad said:

I adore you as the sun and the moon and the stars;
As the earth and the life-giving sea;
As the father you are to us all.

Then he added, "Forgive me, but I cannot adore you as a god."

"What have you been learning?" his father growled.

"What every future king must know," the teacher said.
"He is learning the arts and sciences and scriptures."

"I am also learning what every future king must never forget," Prahlad said. "To be humble."

"And how are you learning this?" his father demanded.

"By worshipping Lord Vishnu. When I fix my thoughts
on him, he fills me with joy."

The king's face grew black with fury. It grew red with shame. "I have forbidden it!" he roared. He stood and said:

I am the lord of the three worlds;
The lord of heaven and earth and hell;
The great Hiranyakasipu.

He liked the way his voice echoed in the throne room. The way light glinted from his golden robes.

His guards looked proud to be serving such a powerful king. The teacher bowed in fright.

Prahlad also bowed, but not in fright. He bowed with respect. "Forgive me, Father," he said, "but there are beings more powerful than you. There are the gods. There is the great Vishnu – he of the blue skin and four arms, he of the peaceful gaze. He alone is the source of your power."

The king pointed at Prahlad and told the guards, "Put this boy to death!"

They took Prahlad back to the forest. Here he sat calmly under a tree. The guards drew their swords and Prahlad fixed his thoughts on Lord Vishnu. The lord filled Prahlad with joy. When the guards fell on him, their swords passed through his body without harm.

The teacher reported this magic to the king.

"Bring deadly serpents," the king ordered.

The guards set loose serpents but Vishnu filled their hearts with fear. Their fangs broke. The serpents fled.

"Bring wild elephants!" the king ordered.

The guards let loose wild elephants. They trampled Prahlad underfoot. He rose unharmed. Vishnu filled the elephants' hearts with fear as well. Their tusks broke and the elephants also fled.

The guards threw Prahlad from a cliff. He landed as if on

moss. They threw him into a fire. He stepped out unscathed. The teacher gave him a goblet of poison, but Vishnu changed the poison into nectar. Now the teacher fled. Prahlad walked back to the city and once more entered the palace. The guards followed him but kept their distance. Evening shadows were filling the throne room. The sun was about to set. This time the king's voice did not echo when he said:

I am the lord of the three worlds;
The lord of heaven and earth and hell;
The great Hiranyakasipu.

"What is the source of your power?" the king asked.

"It is the same as your own," Prahlad said. "None other than Vishnu himself. His power is in everything. He is everywhere."

"Is he in this pillar?" Drawing his sword, the king approached a marble pillar near his throne. "If your lord is not in here, I shall kill you myself!" Hiranyakasipu struck the pillar with his sword.

The veined marble cracked. Fire spurted like blood from the veins. The pillar fell away to reveal Vishnu. Yet he did not look like the lord – he of the blue skin and four arms, he of the peaceful gaze. The creature that stepped from the pillar looked grotesque. From the waist down, it was a man. From the waist up, it was a lion. It advanced on the king with its fangs bared.

"I am favoured by the gods," the king declared. "I told them, 'Let me not be killed by a man or a beast or a god.'"

"I am called Nara-Sinha, the man-lion," the creature said. "I am neither man nor beast nor god."

Vishnu's trickery enraged the king. He raised his sword and attacked. The sword struck Nara-Sinha's iron claws and fell to the ground.

"I need no weapon," the king declared. "I told the gods,

191

'Let me not be killed during day or night.'"

"The sun has set," Nara-Sinha roared. He circled the darkening room. "It is twilight: neither day nor night." Nara-Sinha grasped the king by the throat and lifted him.

The guards, safe behind pillars, watched helplessly.

Prahlad, safe near the throne, closed his eyes and covered his ears.

Nara-Sinha carried the king toward the balcony. The man-lion sat on a bench in the wide doorway and laid the king across his thighs.

The king's head fell back and he gasped. "I said to the gods, 'Let me not be killed either inside or outside my house.'"

"We are on the threshold," Nara-Sinha said. "Neither inside nor out." At last, on the threshold of the balcony, in the fading light of twilight, Nara-Sinha the man-lion disemboweled the king.

Nara-Sinha tossed the pieces aside. He approached Prahlad and sat on the throne. "Ask me for a boon," Nara-Sinha commanded.

"When Lord Vishnu fills me with joy," Prahlad said humbly, "I have all I need."

"You must ask for a boon!"

"Then please purify my father of his sins."

"To think that even demons have such sons!" Nara-Sinha declared. His mane shook when he laughed. "So be it. Now you must reign as king of the demons." At this, Nara-Sinha rose from the throne and Prahlad took his rightful place.

The city began to move. It burrowed down through the seabed into the earth, and the mountains bowed low. It rose up through the sea and waves flung spray at the clouds. Prahlad's subjects cheered. Then, while the city sailed through the air, Vishnu led Hiranyakasipu back to heaven and the gods rained flowers on the sea.

"Guest from India," my paternal grandmother, Bhagirathi, is interviewed on radio by Cornelia Clark, a grade six student at Daniel Webster School.
– Staff Photo by Al Carlino for a local newspaper in 1955–56

PART THREE

Amma, My Mother

My mother, Lakshmi, with me shortly after I was born in March of 1956.

Always Remember That I Loved You

Two nights before my mother finally left us, I dreamt that she had died. I also dreamt that I had cried. Alone. And how had she died? I forgot this in the act of waking, an act that induces amnesia much as the shock of birth apparently does – those unwilling passages from darkness to light that erase everything we knew in the womb and much else we learn in sleep.

"It is good to dream such things," she said. After I told her about her death. Not about my tears. "It will make you strong."

I was nine going on ten. I had no idea why I should be strong.

It was December 1965, our last Christmas as a family although we didn't know this when we'd converged for the holidays. My mother was teaching at Clemson University in South Carolina. She'd come all the way to Kingston, Ontario, for this visit. Not home; simply to visit. My father was teaching at the Royal Military College. Like her, he taught engineering. Unlike her, he enjoyed research and spent long hours in his lab. He lived in a basement apartment to cut costs so that I could attend a boarding school in Ottawa. The following spring, I would refuse to return there. In all, I spent a month of grade five in the infirmary, mainly with colds. I used that quiet place as a haven to escape both day boys and boarders. They were sons of businessmen and diplomats, these boys. The cream of the crop. For years, until it no longer mattered, I thought of them as the scum on top.

I don't remember what gifts my parents gave me that Christmas. I do remember the tree. My father had snuck it downstairs while I'd been playing with the son of the French-speaking family upstairs. I decorated that tree with lights we had bought for my first Christmas in Canada three years earlier: Canadian Tire lights that were now too large for a tree that was small enough for a basement flat. And with mirror balls in red, gold, silver and green. Mainly silver, like the mirror in my magic robot game.

It was a board game that I often played alone, a present from the family upstairs. You placed the robot in a notched circle on the left and turned him until his wand pointed at a question on the overlaid chart: "Who wrote *A Tale of Two Cities?*" Then you guessed the answer. To check if you were correct, you picked the robot out of his notched circle and placed him on a mirror to the right. He spun magically and came to rest with his wand pointing at the answer: "Charles Dickens." I suspected that there was a magnet under the mirror, but I never took the board apart to find out. I suspected this because if I nudged him toward an incorrect answer he resisted. When I let go, he spun past the correct one, but he always returned to it like the needle of a compass finding north. Not true north; magnetic north.

Seated on the floor near the tree, I was playing with this game (learning all the answers) when the bedroom door slammed. It was late Saturday afternoon. My father was at his skating rink, an indoor rink across from RMC. I opened the door to find my mother flinging clothes into a suitcase. She pressed the lid shut as tightly as her lips were pursed.

Finally she said, "I am not staying in this place another minute." While she hurried from bedroom to bathroom, then scanned the living room for anything she might have forgotten, I cried. She was leaving because I'd done something wrong. What I'd done, I didn't know. I also cried because we had tickets (only two – one for her, one for me) to see *My Fair Lady*, the movie, on Sunday night. They were expensive tickets she had bought in advance at either the Hyland or the Biltmore, theatres on Princess Street. The tickets were in her purse, but I said nothing. A few years later, when I mentioned them, she said, "You should have told me."

Now she phoned for a cab to take her to the bus terminal. She planned to take the bus to Toronto and, from there, fly back to the States. I cried while following her to the foot of the basement stairs. From here I watched her climb. From the top, with her hand on the knob of the back door, she said, "Always remember that I loved you." I phoned my father. I even heard him being paged. At least I remember it this way. He sounded annoyed when he came to the phone, but I was used to this because he often sounded annoyed. "She's going," I said through my tears. "She's going by bus." Half an hour later, he was home. I don't remember what I dreamt that night. I do remember running the kitchen tap for a drink of water, ice cold. Later I awoke with a cough. "Why did you run the tap so long?" he demanded. I had no idea.

2

A FEW YEARS LATER, referring to that day, my mother said, "Your father came to the bus terminal." She didn't say whether he'd asked her to stay, and it wasn't the sort of thing I could ask him. There wasn't much I could ask him unless it was about art or history, especially Indian history and his part in the

Independence movement. But I asked her why she'd cut her visit short. "He would not talk to me," she said. "I came all the way to see you, and he would not even talk to me." I was in my mid-teens now. I didn't understand why a man would refuse to talk to his own wife. I didn't understand this until I settled down, finally, at twenty-seven. This, after having learned to enjoy living alone. By then I would be more like my father than I'd thought possible. Better not to talk, though, than fight: a lesson that I'm still trying to unlearn.

Too many times, when my mother had visited us before that Christmas of *My Fair Lady*, I'd hidden in my room with the door closed while my parents had fought. During one of their battles, when I'd been eight, my father's watch had smashed against a wall. The watch was gold-coloured and rectangular, a 1950s model with Roman numerals. I crept out to claim the watch for myself. Later, I took it apart to see why it had stopped; I kept the workings until I grew tired of looking at them. I knew that I could never repair this watch. Only grown-ups could repair watches. They could repair anything.

Spring 1969. It might have been 1970. I don't remember, largely because this was the longest my father and I lived in the same city: Kingston again, after a year in the States, in eastern Pennsylvania, where I learned about Moravian culture. So much of what I do remember, I remember because we moved so much, usually once a year. My mother was also back from the States and now living in a borough of Toronto called Downsview. She was teaching at Atkinson, the engineering college of York University. One day I came home (I was in grade eight or nine) and found my father also home. I was a latchkey child although we weren't called this, perhaps because the term hadn't yet been coined. "Your mother's at the bus terminal," he said. "I'll drop you off." And there she was, with her suitcase again.

"I came for the divorce," she explained. "We were at the courthouse all afternoon." Now she was on her way back to Toronto. The divorce was more a relief than a surprise – this news, and it explained why my guidance counselor at school invited me for monthly chats. For years, she had talked about divorcing my father, when she'd railed about him to me, always when he'd been out. She'd even frightened me by saying, "I will shoot him. I will take a gun and shoot him." After a while I'd stopped taking either threat seriously: the shooting or the divorce.

Seated on a wooden bench, while we waited for her bus, we chatted about school. She watched me while I read the board of arrivals and departures. In school, I was one of the few boys at the top of my grade. I was going to be a physicist when I grew up. I'd read every biography of Albert Einstein in our branch of the public library, and I couldn't wait to grow up. If not a physicist, then a magician. I'd also read biographies of Harry Houdini. In my favourite scene, he comes to his mother, asks her to close her eyes, and pours gold coins into her lap. He'd become more than a good magician by then: he could escape from anything.

Next we chatted about my birthday, which was coming up. I may not have had two parents, but I knew how to get anything I wanted from them. Anything but love, but I never thought to ask for this. It should have come naturally, I thought. I'd invented my own rules for the workings of families. Rules like: honour thy children. This means (a) a mother shouldn't abandon her son, and (b) if she does, she shouldn't expect to be loved. I often thought these words: *should* and *shouldn't*. I used them all too often in the years that followed. For now I couldn't make my father happy, and I couldn't make my mother come back but, like Houdini, I could work magic: I could transform guilt into gifts.

One Christmas, I'd asked her in a letter for not one gift but two. "You cannot live in a dream world," she'd written in reply. Why not? With so many things, who needed parents? And I had many things. I didn't simply own books: I owned a library complete with encyclopedias of history and art. And toys? Such toys. One Christmas my father had taken me to New York City and, at Macy's department store, I'd bought a battery-operated Aston Martin: metallic grey, with rotating licence plates, a bullet-proof shield, wing-mounted machine guns and even an ejection seat. I no longer played with it, but I treasured it. I no longer played with it because I'd packed all my toys into their boxes. At twelve, I'd decided that my childhood was over. Now, at thirteen or fourteen, I played games like Broadside and Stratego, Scrabble and Monopoly. And with a physics set. I owned not one microscope but two. Best of all, I had a stamp collection.

And so for my coming birthday I asked my mother for not one album but two: a new, larger world album and one for the American stamps I'd begun collecting the year my father and I had lived in the States. That was the year he'd finished his doctorate, something that she'd done years before him; a fact she'd never let him forget. This time she didn't say, "You cannot live in a dream world." She promised both albums. How could she refuse?

The last thing she said before I left her, still on the bench with her suitcase, was, "Always remember that I loved you." It would become a line of our song, our own secret song. And, just as I'd once stopped believing that she would carry out her threats against my father, so I now stopped believing that she loved me.

Why did you leave? What did I do wrong?
Always remember that I loved you.

3

During grades nine and ten, I saw my mother three or four times a year: once or twice in summer, once at Easter, always at Christmas. When my father and I moved to Vancouver, this routine stopped for grades eleven and twelve. It re-established itself when I returned east to attend Carleton University. Not to study physics, though. I was still fascinated by the known forces of the universe: electromagnetic, gravitational, strong nuclear and weak nuclear; by Einstein's musing that if these forces were but manifestations of a single force, we might have mathematical proof for the existence of one God. But to become a physicist would be to follow my family into the sciences, and I'd decided scientists and engineers cared more about things than people: about formulae more than children. Another lesson I would unlearn.

My visiting her was a grudging duty, but it also provided an escape: first from a father I could rarely please and, later, from a university residence emptied for the holidays. He and I had finally grown apart. We'd succumbed to the magnetic law that like repels like. I suspect that he thought I loved her more than I loved him. How could I? The mother I visited was not the mother I remembered from our time in India. That mother had dressed me in costumes: a sheriff's vest; the grey-green uniform of an officer in the Indian Air Force; a soldier's red tunic with black trousers; even pink coveralls with a steam engine she'd embroidered on the bib. These last two, she had made herself. That mother took me to Cantonment, the old British military district of Bangalore, for juice in tea rooms. There I'd watched old men pour coffee into saucers, blow on the coffee before sipping, and smack their lips. That mother had been beautiful; she'd been strong. She'd worn saris, and I'd called her by an Indian term of endearment:

Amma, which means mother. Now I called her Mom. She'd forsaken her saris for western clothes and they didn't suit her. She was growing fat. She was growing dark. She was growing insufferable. She ate dry toast for breakfast, Quaker Harvest Crunch for lunch, Swanson TV dinners at night.

I especially remember these because I also ate them. My favourite dinner was the Salisbury steak, which came with vanilla macaroon pudding. You peeled away the hot aluminum foil from the neatly crimped edge of the aluminum tray; cleaned your glasses, which had fogged from the sudden rise of steam; and you ate, burning your tongue.

And every year, she bought a different exercise machine. One was a pink bench that promised to vibrate away her fat. I don't remember the others: vinyl pads and crimped tubes and springs that rocked or stretched and always collapsed for easy storage. I grew to loathe them because they reminded me that I was also overweight: chubby by twelve, fat by fifteen.

At sixteen, thanks to walking uphill and down in Vancouver, I grew mercifully thin. According to her, I looked simply dashing in my army cadet and army reserve uniforms: the blue and green MacKenzie tartan of the Seaforth Highlanders of Canada, the scarlet tunic and black bearskin of the Governor General's Foot Guards. My father had suggested that I join cadets to get out of the house; I'd later decided to join the reserves. I liked being part of a greater whole. My mother liked the uniforms. Sometimes our visits were pleasant, almost fun. We went to movies like *Fiddler on the Roof*, which needed expensive tickets, bought in advance, at the University Theatre on Toronto's Bloor Street. We visited her few friends, like Nalla S. and her husband, who were Sinhalese. We played board games. As time wore on and my patience wore thin, we did less together. My mother slept; I watched TV. I went to movies alone, movies that a young man couldn't watch with his mother: movies like *A Clockwork Orange*. I even walked the streets of downtown in search of the perfect clubhouse sandwich. Anything to avoid her complaints about work – first at York, then at a high school for gifted students.

She'd switched from engineering to education and our song had a new line: "You see, I am not well." She said it so often that I stopped believing her.

"It's all in your mind," I said. "They," meaning her colleagues, "aren't really after you." And it was in her mind, more than I suspected.

Her group therapy, her weekly sessions with a psychologist – I couldn't take any of these seriously even though, during my third year at Carleton, I also began visiting a psychologist. I spent nine months of that year (a symbolic nine months) in group therapy. But it never occurred to me how inextricably my life was braided with hers: how I also fell ill when I was frightened or unhappy. I learned more: why I felt responsible for everything and everyone; why I tried so hard to be perfect. Best of all, I learned the self-inflicted tyranny of those words *should* and *shouldn't*. My doctor's name was Powers, of all things. If anyone in the group looked to him for answers, he would smile. "I'm not Solomon," he would say. To me he might just as well have said, "I'm no magic robot."

In the summer between my third and fourth years, I travelled to Switzerland and Austria, then studied in France. This was the happiest summer of my life: afternoons at our college behind Invalides; evenings debating life under the Arc de Triomphe; weekends at Chartres, Saint-Denis, the chateaux of the Loire. And always the company of women: Americans named Linda and Carol and Kathy who taught me little about love and much about being at ease. Kathy best of all, even if she was engaged to a professional baseball player – Kathy, who taught me the lesson every young man must learn: be yourself.

But all summers end, even in Paris.

The visits to my mother began again in the fall, continued over winter, stretched into spring. I watched her eat her Harvest Crunch and TV dinners, but I couldn't ignore the paper plates overflowing in the garbage or the few dishes in her kitchen sink. I half-heartedly cleaned up and gladly agreed when she asked me to stop. In the end, I couldn't even go into her kitchen. This was the day I found the worms. Tiny worms flopped on mouldy dishes and crusted plates. Tiny worms curled their ribbed bodies into themselves. Tiny worms wriggled on the tea-stained aluminum.

"There's something in the sink," I told her.

"I know," she said. She'd been lying on the sofa all afternoon while I'd been out. "I sprinkle them with Ajax," she said, "but it does no good. They keep coming back."

4

SPRING 1977. The week of my convocation, my father phoned to say, "I've been on this continent for twenty years. I've waited till you got your first degree. Now I'm going home." He was living in a motel in Lillooet, B.C., inland from Vancouver.

Before he left, he sent me my twenty-first birthday present: enough money to start graduate school or travel for a year. I chose travel. I planned to spend the coming fall and winter in India because a new question had surfaced in my mind: a question that I'd ignored during fifteen years of trying to induce amnesia, as though erasing India from my mind could somehow make me more Canadian than I felt. The question was, simply, "Am I Indian or Canadian?" No one could answer this question for me: not a doctor named Powers, who was no Solomon; not any magic robot.

You see, *I am not well.*

It's all in your *mind.*

5

FOR MOST OF MY first summer as a Bachelor of Arts with Honours, I avoided Toronto. I couldn't avoid my mother's weekly phone calls though, always on Sunday. One weekend she didn't call. She was supposed to be visiting relatives in the States, but I knew that she would still call. Instead of feeling relieved that she hadn't, I worried. I phoned the relatives. "She never came," they said. I phoned her friends in Toronto. "Your mother is in the hospital," Nalla S. told me. "The Clarke Institute." She said it with a significance that I didn't grasp. "What do you suppose a son should do?"

I had no idea. I even resented the implication I was a less than dutiful son. I soon forgave her this, once I was no longer sure what I heard. Had she meant to be critical, or had I simply heard what I'd least wanted to hear?

The train brought me into Toronto in the early morning. I bought time over breakfast at Union Station. Then I found my way to the Clarke Institute. I don't remember what floor the receptionist sent me to, but I soon learned that such things were important. The floor in a psychiatric hospital was important because it said much about the person on it. My mother was on either eleven or twelve.

In the waiting room, I tried ignoring the patients. There was no point ignoring them, though, because they ignored me. They wandered in; they sat on vinyl chairs; they shuffled cards and smoked; they wandered out. By the time a doctor came for me, the patients were no longer people; they were things. They were slippers down at the heels, ashtrays full of butts, the shuffle and slap of cards. They were bathrobes, blue and green plaid. Not like the MacKenzie tartan of the Seaforth Highlanders; dark like The Black Watch.

The doctor took me into the hallway and told me the problem. He kept to generalities, but one thing stayed in my mind: "She's anxious about your going all the way to India." I said nothing because I found this hard to believe. "We'll give her a day pass," he said.

It wasn't much of a visit. Finally entering the waiting room, she seemed upset that I'd come. She said little besides (in the elevator, while I watched the numbers decrease), "How can you see me like this?" Once on the bus, in a side-ways-facing seat behind the driver, she cried. She cried without making a sound. I sat across the aisle and tried to look out the window behind her. I pretended that I wasn't with her. It hardly mattered, though. Just like the patients in the waiting room, the other passengers ignored us. They ignored the fat, dark woman who cried without making a sound and the young man, too young to understand. I don't remember if we had a conversation after reaching her apartment. That evening she made her own way back to the hospital, and I returned by bus to Ottawa.

October of 1977 found me in South India. I was living with my father again, in a rented farmhouse on Debur Road that stood between Debur village and Nanjangud town. It was a short ride by diesel train to Mysore, where he worked at NIE, the National Institute of Engineering. It was a longer ride by steam train to Bangalore, my hometown: a city, in fact. Once a month, I went there to stay with my paternal grandmother and visit my Uncle Joga-Rao's family. He was one of my two maternal uncles and he lived in the same house that he'd bought from my mother shortly before I'd been born. He wasn't a gypsy like my father. This is what my mother had always called him – a gypsy – and she hadn't meant it kindly. By now, my father and I were working toward our own form of peace: uneasy but a peace nonetheless.

One day in November, as soon as I arrived at my uncle's house, his wife, my Aunt Rukmini, said, "Something has happened to your mother." Rukmini said that Joga-Rao hadn't been able to tell me about it because it had shaken him. Between a telegram and a letter, both from Toronto, although not from my mother, Rukmini and I reconstructed what had happened.

Two weeks before, my mother's building superintendent had been passing her apartment. Purely by chance, he'd tried the knob and found the door unlocked. Perhaps he'd often tried the knob when he'd passed this door because my mother was known to be a fearful woman. Wherever she'd lived, she'd asked superintendents to put an extra chain on her door. He'd entered the apartment and found her lying on the sofa. She'd taken an overdose of sleeping pills.

This should have been the end but it wasn't. So many times during the next few years, I would wish that it had been the end. He'd found her alive. An ambulance had rushed her to Mount Sinai Hospital. This was when my uncle had received the telegram and, shortly afterwards, the letter from one of Amma's few friends. My mother wouldn't be there for long, though: not in Mount Sinai or even Toronto. She had decided to visit India.

In the fifteen years between the autumn of 1962, when she'd brought me to my father in Canada – in the years between then and this, my first India trip – the three of us had lived in seven cities in four provinces and states. We'd sometimes lived together, a family straining at the weak nuclear forces binding it, more often we'd lived apart, and too often we'd lived alone. Now we were converging in our homeland, just as we'd converged in Kingston that Christmas I'd dreamt she had died. Only days before she reached India in December, a jumbo jet crashed into the sea while it approached Bombay Airport. She wasn't on this plane. So many times during the next few years, I would wish that she had been on it.

6

Why did you leave? What did I do wrong?
Always remember that I loved you.
You see, I am not well.
It's all in your *mind.*
There's something in the sink.
I know.

Guardsman Ven Begamudré of the Governor General's Foot Guards in Ottawa in August of 1974.

DEATH CALLS

"I HAVE RECEIVED a death call," my grandmother said. It was the morning of Tuesday, January 17, 1978. "Your Aunt Mani has died during the night."

We took an autorickshaw, a motorized three-wheeled vehicle, to Mani's house in Jayanagar district. She lay on a mat in the middle of the main room. Someone had arranged a garland so that it outlined her head and shoulders. She looked asleep.

In the middle of the night, she suffers a heart attack and calls to her youngest son, Ravi. She tells him she is about to die and asks him to call for a doctor. The doctor arrives too late.

Her estranged husband, Srinivas, and my cousin Radha wept quietly in a back room. Ravi wailed. The dark crescents under his eyes looked black. He hadn't slept since Mani had awoken him. When I tried to clasp Radha's arm, she said something I didn't understand. Her children, Janaki and Haymanth, also cried, but not constantly like the grown-ups. Soon Janaki and Haymanth ran about the house, even about the body, while people came and went. The grown-ups endured my grandmother's conversation though she wasn't part of the family. Mani was one of her three stepchildren, after all – almost her age – and they'd had little contact even while my grandfather had been alive. My grandmother had done her duty by bringing me, and she left soon after.

I sat in a corner of the main room to listen and watch. It all seemed so practical that I decided never to attend a Canadian funeral. They seemed theatrical in comparison; even the corpse was made up. This would become an almost inviolable rule in the eleven years that followed, but then few people I knew would die in that time. Now there were rituals to be observed, farewells to express, and grief to overcome. But most of this would have to wait. The main thing was to cremate Mani's body before its fluids drained into the stomach and the stomach burst. We waited all morning for the van that would take the body to the crematorium. Mani's younger sister, my Aunt Ratna, was now in charge. No one said so, but it was clear: the presence of a senator from New Delhi ensured that everything would go smoothly.

The corporation van, so called because Bangalore is a city corporation, was high and black. Its sides were made of glass because death here wasn't something to hide. The men of the immediate family loaded the body into the van. My father was conspicuously absent. Because only men could go to the crematorium, four of them climbed into the van. When one asked if I wanted to go with them, I said no. I would have felt self-conscious with the others. Not a trespasser like my grandmother, but still out of place. And so I went in someone's car to the crematorium at a spot with the innocent sounding name of Wilson Gardens, where I joined the others.

The crematorium was huge, a concrete and metal structure: blocky concrete surrounding a high, metal roof – curved like a Quonset hut but smooth, not corrugated. Inside, attendants placed the body on a low, silver- coloured trolley. The electric doors of the furnace opened, and an attendant pushed the trolley inside. It tilted so the body could slide down between gas jets. He retracted the trolley and closed the huge doors. Another attendant twisted dials on a control panel. The crematorium began to throb. Someone told me that the furnace could reach 1,200 degrees Fahrenheit; that it could reduce a body to ashes in twenty to forty minutes. It all seemed so practical to me.

The services for Mani would be held in ten days, two Fridays from now. I planned to attend if I was back in Bangalore from Debur Road.

Two days after Mani's death, I found myself returning to my grandmother's house. Perhaps from a movie; I don't remember. I do remember the vision. It wasn't really a vision, though some people claim that I have them because we Pisces are supposed to be prescient. I preferred to think of these visions as flights of imagination – because I spent so much time dwelling on the past that I couldn't help wondering what the future might hold. Even as I walked up my grandmother's street, I saw this:

While I am out, my father arrives from his farmhouse on Debur Road. He comes to my grandmother's house to wash and change before going on to Mani's house. He suffers a heart attack. I turn the corner towards my grandmother's house and find people gathered at both gates: the one marked ANANDA for her favourite son, a merchant mariner; the other one marked BEGAMUDRE for me. The people in the main room part to let me through, and I see my father. He lies on the narrow bed in my grandmother's room. Someone has arranged a garland so that it outlines his head and shoulders. Radha weeps quietly in a back room; Ravi wails. Janaki and Haymanth also cry, but not constantly. Soon they run about, even into my grandmother's room, and out again. She chats with Ratna while we wait for the corporation van to arrive. I begin to weep.

But when I turned the corner, no one stood at the gate. My grandmother sat reading in the main room. I didn't tell her about the vision, of course, if that's what it was.

The next morning, I went to Aunt Mani's house once again. Her other two children, my cousins Krishna and Gita, had finally reached Bangalore. I hadn't seen them in over fifteen years, but it didn't feel like a reunion.

There were rituals to be observed. None of the immediate family could go outside, and they had to take a bath every day. Their father, Srinivas, was not as orthodox as the others. He shared an autorickshaw with me back to Malleswaram; back to my maternal Uncle Joga-Rao's house. Here Srinivas decided to come inside. I listened, embarrassed for him, while he tried to exonerate himself to Joga-Rao's wife, my Aunt Rukmini, and to my mother. I listened while he tried to convince them – more likely, himself – that he wasn't to blame over Mani's difficulties after he had left her. My mother seemed not to care.

After he left, my mother and I sat in the verandah, and she spoke as if to herself. She wore saris now, the first she had worn in nearly ten years – since she had cut her long hair and westernized herself; since I had stopped calling her Amma and started calling her Mom. Today her sari was yellow. She said she had applied to enter an ashram called Ramakrishna. At the interview earlier in the week, she had learned that it didn't want her for her teaching skills. It wanted her to raise funds. She clung to one last hope: an honorary teaching position at Rishi Valley School, the boarding school my father had attended as a boy. Joga-Rao intended to take her there for the interview next week. She had arrived in India barely a month before, but she was already thinking of returning to Canada. Britain planned to revoke the passports of citizens living abroad, she said. She feared that Canada might do the same. I didn't know about Britain, but I thought I understood Canada well enough to know that it would never do such a thing.

Nothing I said could reassure her.

When I suggested we go for a walk, she fretted until Rukmini cajoled her. *"Yem-Lakshmi?"* Rukmini demanded. "Show him the house!" Then, to me: "You remember your house, hah?"

We had called it the Coloured House. On special occasions our servant, Mary, had replaced the regular light bulbs with coloured ones, blue and green. For many months back then, I'd been unable to walk because of a rash. It was the same rash that plagued me now and kept my visits to Bangalore short: a rash that demanded regular baths followed by much ointment – both then and now. And yet those days had been the happiest of my life, for this is how I remembered them. I'd seen the house only two months before, when Joga-Rao and Rukmini's son, my cousin Sinu, had taken me past it. Now it was like seeing it again for the first time since I'd left India. The house was red and off-white, and someone had added a second storey. The garden I'd played in as a boy was smaller than I remembered it. But the coconut palms had grown, and their branches had spread.

"So much has changed," my mother said, turning away from the house. "Prices have shot up, but I think I can get a job. I was a good teacher once."

"You still are," I said.

"I am not well."

"It's all in your mind."

On our way back, she stopped to visit a friend, a woman many years older than her whom I couldn't remember having known. Inside this house, my mother showed me the study. "It was her husband's," my mother said. "He died about the time you were born." Something looked amiss among the items on the desk: the pen lying beside the inkwell, the open book. "It hasn't changed," my mother said. "Not since the day he died."

"Everything is as he left it," the friend said from behind us. "I have disturbed nothing." She looked almost proud while she told me this.

When we left, my mother made *namaskaar*, the ritual of bowing reverently over clasped hands. "You also make *namaskaar*," she said.

I looked at her in scorn. I wore a *kurtha* – a long, high necked shirt; loose trousers called pyjamas; and Bata sandals. People called me Babu, as they had when I'd been a boy, but I was no longer Indian. The long days at the farmhouse on Debur Road had taught me this. Without really looking for the answer to a question – Am I Indian or Canadian? – I had found it somehow: I was neither; I was both.

Back at Joga-Rao's house again, my mother and I sat on the step. To our right stood a scraggly pine tree, the tallest in the front garden. Fifteen years ago, it had been my first Christmas tree, small enough to grow in an earthenware pot. Our servant, Mary, had tied ribbons on it; my mother had given a party. It had been her way of preparing me for Canada. One of many ways, some more successful than others: an inflatable Santa Claus, a boiled egg I'd been unable to eat. My mother didn't speak of that Christmas, though. She still spoke of how things had changed and how prices had gone up. I finally grew annoyed at her; at my inability to help her.

"I am not well," she said. "Rukmini–"

"Why don't you listen to her?" I asked. "She's right, you know. Don't stay in the house all day. Things can't be that bad. Are you taking your pills?"

She toyed with a handkerchief, folded it, refolded it, and tucked it into the waist of her sari. The sari didn't suit her, though, just as the western clothes hadn't suited her.

I rose to go. I told her that I planned to leave for Debur Road on Sunday to get more ointment; that I might visit her again before I left. In any case, I hoped to be back in Bangalore for the services for Mani.

"She had a difficult life," my mother said. "Now she is at peace."

—※※—

SATURDAY, JANUARY 21ST, four days after Mani's death. Cecil B. DeMille's *The Ten Commandments* began at three o'clock. It was playing at a theatre in the Chickpet district, near the bus and railway stations. I'd seen the movie – on the day I'd finished high school, in Vancouver – but I picked this theatre because, like the movie, it was old. I wouldn't have to stand in line for long to buy a ticket. The seats were hard, the floor rickety. Ceiling fans on long rods moved smoke from the lower seats up to the balcony. The sturdiest part of the theatre was the verandah wrapped around the second floor. This is where I was, during the second intermission, at five-thirty, when I saw my grandmother. She wasn't wandering through the crowds at ground level. She knew I wouldn't be down there.

"Here," she said. Her arm was outstretched, her hand closing with the palm down. "Your Joga-Rao Uncle telephoned. He asked me to bring you to his house." She could say nothing more while we elbowed our way down the steps and through the crowd at ground level. Then: "I think your mother is no more."

"You think?" I shouted it, partly to be heard above the street noise. "Grandma, yes or no?"

"Don't get excited," she said. "She has set herself on fire like her own mother did."

"Is she dead?" I was trying not to shout.

"Maybe very little life is left."

We searched along the narrow, crowded street for an autorickshaw. I couldn't believe it. Not that my mother might be dead; the *Don't get excited.*

An autorickshaw pulled up and stopped with its single front wheel against the curb. Passengers dismounted and paid their fare. A man and his wife were waiting to get in, but my grandmother pulled the couple away. "Death call," she told them. "Death call," she told the driver. The couple nodded, the driver shrugged, and we climbed into the back. Then we were off.

"What a silly girl!" my grandmother said. Then: "Your Joga-Rao Uncle asked me to bring you in a taxi. I waited for an hour after going inside the theatre. The usher helped me look for you." And then, annoyed: "Where should I find a taxi?"

The autorickshaw tilted while it raced around Kempegowda Circle. I stopped listening to her. I was angry because I was afraid; angry because my mother had once again betrayed me just as she had, long ago, by leaving me with my father. It had been Christmas; I'd been nine going on ten. And just as Srinivas had done over Aunt Mani's death, I kept reminding myself I was not to blame for anything that had happened to her.

"So many people in the house," my grandmother said. "What were all of them doing?"

I felt sad for Joga-Rao's children. But more than anger and sadness, I felt fear. I imagined my mother wrapped in bandages and lying on her deathbed; imagined her pleading for my forgiveness. "Please, God," I thought, "let her be dead." I thought this.

The autorickshaw rattled up Margosa Road into Malleswaram district. At Joga-Rao's house, we found a man waiting at the gate. He wore a tweed jacket and looked as if he'd just come from work. I sounded much too blunt when I asked, "Who are you?"

"The Institute registrar," he replied. "Nanjan-Rao is my name." He already knew mine. My grandmother entered the house, but he led me around the side to the back. To our right ran a concrete fence that separated Joga-Rao's house from its neighbour to the north. I could sense someone watching me from a window of the next house but I thought nothing of it. I was used to people watching me: the Canadian boy, so lucky he is.

Even as I cleared the corner, I saw Joga-Rao seated on a stone bench. He wore a blue three-piece suit, a white shirt, and a red tie. I had never seen him dressed so well. He sat turned towards the back door without looking at it. He sat with his head down, his shoulders hunched. His clasped hands sagged between his knees, and he held a cigarette. He didn't appear to be grieving. I must have appeared the same to him. The grief would come later. "Ah, there you are," he said. He looked down again. He didn't have to tell me where to look.

My mother lay on the concrete behind the open back door. The blanket and small rug covering her were partly burned. She lay with her head towards the garden; with her right arm outstretched as if crying for help. She had spent so much of her life crying for help. The ruby bangle on her wrist was charred. Her forearm was swollen and black. The skin on her forearm had split open.

Fascinated by the arm, I took a step towards her. "When did it happen?" I asked.

"Between three and four," he said.

I asked, as though projecting my voice to reach an audience behind me, "Was it a quick death?"

"Oh," he said, "yes." He gestured for me to sit beside him, but I remained standing.

My grandmother came around the side of the house. She made some disjointed comments – "I found a taxi. You are all fine?" – and then left. I was glad to see her go. She was even less a part of my mother's family than she was of her own.

Joga-Rao seemed to sense my questions, what few I allowed myself, before I asked them. He had not been home when it had happened. Nor had anyone else. My mother had bided her time, or chosen it well.

After lunch, Joga-Rao and his sister, Lakshmi, listen to a violin recital on the radio. Later he will say, "She seemed her normal self."

As a girl, my mother had played the violin and even won a gold medal. Once, in Toronto, I had watched her play. I'd been in my early teens then. She'd sat cross-legged on the living room floor, held the violin in her lap like a cello, and played a few bars for me. I'd found the music impossible to follow: foreign, dissonant. She'd sensed my disinterest and put the violin away. In all my visits after that, she never again took that violin out.

At three o'clock, Joga-Rao, Rukmini, and their five children prepare to leave for Mount Carmel College. They're going to an exhibit of science projects. The eldest girl, Bujji, has won a prize for hers. It's a bed-wetting alarm. The third girl, Rani, complains of a stomach ache. She is like her Aunt Lakshmi, not only musical but also prone to mood swings. Rani wants to stay home but Lakshmi persuades her to go. Rukmini tries to cajole Lakshmi into coming with them but she refuses. "Babu might come this afternoon," she says. Rukmini believes her.

In fact, I didn't know whether anyone except my grandmother knew I was at the theatre. Sometimes, in later years, it would matter whether anyone else knew. My mother had also been at a movie when her own mother, the grandmother I never knew, had killed herself. Years later a friend would tell me this is called ritualization.

Someone at Mount Carmel College tells Joga-Rao he's wanted on the phone. It's urgent: a neighbour. She's in tears and can barely speak. He knows Lakshmi is dead. Rukmini refuses to believe it. Still, she takes the children to a friend's house while he hurries back to his own.

From the neighbour's house, Joga-Rao phones for the police. None can come. Morarji Desai, the prime minister, is in Bangalore. Half the force is guarding him while the other half directs traffic along his route. Joga-Rao knows he can't cope with everything that will follow, so he phones three colleagues at his institute. The registrar, Nanjan-Rao, can handle any legal difficulties. A doctor named Suba-Rao can handle medical details. The security officer, a man simply called Raja, will deal with the police.

Nanjan-Rao left me with my uncle and entered the back of the house. A stranger came out. He wore neither a jacket nor a tie. Instead he wore a clean bush shirt above good trousers. He was tall, dark and barrel-chested and his moustache was thick, vaguely military.

"Ah," Joga-Rao said, "there you are."

He didn't introduce Raja and there was little need to introduce me. Everyone knew who I was: the Canadian nephew, the sister's son.

When Raja lifted the upper-left corner of the blanket, Joga-Rao rose and moved forwards. Perhaps he was trying to block my view. Perhaps not.

Lakshmi walks Joga-Rao and his family to the gate. A girl named Viju, the daughter of the neighbour next door, is playing in the front garden of Joga-Rao's house. Both Lakshmi and Viju's mother wave goodbye. Then Lakshmi asks Viju's mother to take

221

the girl home. Lakshmi says she wants to rest. She goes inside and locks the front door.

Some time later, she takes her glasses off. They're bifocals. She places them on the dining table without folding the stems behind the lenses. She always puts her glasses down like this. She goes into the back of the house and closes the connecting door.

In the bathing room, she pours kerosene into a bucket. She douses her sari with the kerosene. She steps from the bathing room, strikes a match, and places the matchbook on the edge of the washstand. It takes only one match. She stands here in this half hallway, half room while she burns. She stands here till she can no longer bear the pain. Then she stumbles, screaming, out the back of the house.

Like the ruby bangle, the thin gold chain around my mother's neck was scorched. Her face was blackened except around the mouth and nose. Here it was red. A line of dried blood trickled from one nostril, a red-black line that vanished somewhere past the right side of her mouth. Her hair looked like shavings of charcoal. Her eyebrows were raised as if in a question; her eyes were closed. Mine kept returning to the split in the skin of her forearm. She looked like a bloated doll tossed onto a rubbish heap. A partly burned doll.

Raja let the blanket fall. It still didn't quite cover the entire arm. The fingers of her right hand, curling, remained in sight. He walked back into the house. The mango leaves strung over the back door for good luck – leaves that had long ago shrivelled in the sun – were also charred. Joga-Rao followed and so did I. Just inside was a small, bare space – a half hallway, half room – with a porcelain washstand. Next to the exposed pipes under the washstand stood a rectangular, one-gallon tin of kerosene, used for lanterns. We looked up.

"Suba-Rao said she was determined," Joga-Rao told Raja. "You see how scorched it is?" The ceiling was black. "He said she must have stood here for a long time, she was so determined."

The neighbours on the south side of Joga-Rao's house have a boy who is crippled. One leg and one arm are deformed, but he can play with the help of a brace and a crutch. He is playing in their back garden when he hears a shriek. A ball of fire hurtles out of Joga-Rao's house. When the boy screams, his parents rush outside. Viju's mother also hears the screams and runs into her own back garden. Viju follows her. "A ball of fire," the grown-ups will later say. The boy's father clambers over the low fence and scoops dirt onto the flames. His wife tosses him a blanket. Viju's mother tosses him a small rug from her clothesline. The boy keeps screaming. Viju is very quiet.

Raja talked to Nanjan-Rao while Joga-Rao and I returned to the bench outside. This time I did sit when he gestured for me to join him. Finally I heard myself say, "Can I have a cigarette?" We sat and smoked. Wind rustled in the few trees in the back garden. It was early evening, the sun was setting beyond houses to the west, and the wind began to die. The only birds in the trees were crows, but I don't remember if they cawed.

"We must remove the body before it grows dark," Joga-Rao said. "Otherwise the monkeys and dogs will come. We must await the police, though."

After a while, I left him. I went around to the front of the house and sat on the step. There was one tree out of place here among the coconut palms and margosas: a scraggly pine, my first ever Christmas tree. Scraggly but so tall now. When a man and woman came through the gate, I edged to the left in case they wanted to enter the verandah. She did but he stopped to speak.

"You are the nephew," he said. I nodded. "And your father?"

"He lives near Nanjangud," I replied. "They were divorced." I didn't know why I said this.

"Oh," he said before entering. "I see."

Neither he nor his wife stayed for long.

I watched the trees: the scraggly pine, two coconut palms at the gate. Even as the moon reached the lower fronds, three men arrived. One, in a brown uniform, was a sub-inspector of police. Another was called the Writer; he wore a shirt and loose pyjama trousers like mine. The third, also in uniform, was a policeman. I entered with them and watched while they went into the back garden with Joga-Rao, Nanjan-Rao, and Raja. The policeman remained out there while the other five re-entered the house. When I wasn't seated at the dining table, I paced into the kitchen, where I drank water from a stainless steel tumbler. Through the window, I could see the policeman seated on the bench. He'd been left to chase away monkeys and dogs that might wander into the garden. None did, though. When I sat, it was at the far end of the dining table from the men. They ignored my mother's glasses, which nobody moved.

The Writer asked questions. Joga-Rao answered only those relating to the family. "Name of deceased? Father's name? Husband's name?" None of the questions really sounded like questions to me. Nanjan-Rao answered others with his tweed arms crossed in front of his tweed chest. Raja watched silently but his presence couldn't be ignored. The Writer repeated the answers to the sub-inspector, who filled in his forms. It took a long time because he kept putting down the answers incorrectly, but protocol had to be observed. It wasn't the Writer's place to fill out forms. He understood legal procedure and spoke English. He dictated. Questions continued. Forms were filled.

I went through the verandah and again sat on the front step. The moon was clearing the tops of the coconut palms at the gate. When a grey taxi finally stopped in front of the house, I went inside.

Raja told the driver and two hired men what to do. They wrapped my mother in another blanket, carried her around the side of the house, and slid her onto the back seat. The taxi left. So did the Writer, the sub-inspector and the policeman. The taxi cost a hundred rupees. Joga-Rao tipped the Writer, the sub-inspector and the policeman. And the men who would deliver my mother to the morgue? Or, rather, her corpse. When I asked, "These tips–?" Joga-Rao said, "It is all right. We can settle everything later on."

Raja understood what I was trying to ask. "It is the only way to deal with such people," he said. "Good thing you are not poor. These policemen are especially good at cheating the poor – saying the family burned the woman themselves and getting bribes so as not to file a false report." He told Joga-Rao, "Tomorrow morning at the morgue?"

Joga-Rao nodded.

Raja and Nanjan-Rao left.

Rukmini arrived first to ensure that the coast was clear. From another room, I heard her ask, "How is he?" She meant me.

I didn't hear most of Joga-Rao's reply; only: "He asked for a cigarette."

Then she made me sit with her in the verandah and insisted on holding my hand. "What a terrible thing to happen, Babu," she said. "In my house. In my house!" Only when Joga-Rao brought the children back, only when they filed past us through the verandah, did she begin to cry. Rani, the girl who had wanted to stay home, also began to cry. Soon Rukmini and the girls prepared supper. Joga-Rao and I sat at the table once more. He had put my mother's glasses away and had closed the door to the back room.

"God is great, Amma," the eldest girl, Bujji, told Rukmini. "Just think, last week both of you were in Tirumala and we were all alone with...her. And on Tuesday you are leaving for Vizag," she told Joga-Rao. He would be receiving a distinguished alumnus award there from his old college. "What if she had done it while you were away? What would we have done?"

During supper someone came to see Joga-Rao about business but Rukmini asked them to leave. I heard her say, "We have had some bad news."

Shortly afterwards, a young man, sent by his parents, arrived. His father, a Dr. A.K. Rao, had been a close friend of my mother. We drove to an all-night telegraph office to send a telegram to my father. It read, "Lakshmi-Bai dead; cremation noon Sunday. If you come, bring ointment. Ven." Joga-Rao also phoned the principal of my father's college in Mysore, the NIE, and asked him to send a message to the farm – in case our telegram didn't arrive. There were no phones on Debur Road.

Ten years before, when my father and I had lived in Pennsylvania, he'd received a message in much the same way. I'd been playing baseball when a stranger asked directions to our apartment. Later, I learned that he was delivering a telegram from my mother's doctor. This was before the divorce so my father was still her next of kin. She needed a hysterectomy, and the surgeon needed my father's permission to operate. The stranger had come all the way from the campus, across town by bus, because we hadn't had a phone. Not then. Not now.

There seemed to be no question of my staying the night in my grandmother's house. For now, at least, I was fully a part of my uncle's family, my mother's side of the family. I left everyone in the front room and went outside to the back.

Someone had thrown more dirt on the blackened concrete; on the blood drying in the dark. I cut down the charred mango leaves and threw them away so that my cousins wouldn't see them. I changed into a *kurtha* and trousers that belonged to Joga-Rao. They were loose, ideal for sleep. I went to bed in the spare room off the dining room, near the half hallway, half room with the scorched ceiling. Everyone else went to bed upstairs. It was past midnight but I couldn't sleep. My skin was dry because I hadn't had my evening bath. I began reading *The Swiss Family Robinson*. At three in the morning, still awake and having read half the book, I went to the kitchen for water. Someone had padlocked the door leading to the back of the house. I fell asleep with the light on.

Before Viju's mother phones Joga-Rao — before she makes her death call — she phones for an ambulance and a doctor. They arrive quickly and leave just as quickly. There is nothing the doctor can do. The crippled boy's parents take him to a distant house. There he finally stops screaming. Viju sits quietly for an hour, then starts to laugh. She keeps laughing about seeing a ball of fire.

And just as I had two nights before my mother had finally left us — just as I had during our last Christmas as a family — I dreamt I was crying. But this time, in this dream, someone sang, "Happy Days Are Here Again." I can't explain this part of the dream. Perhaps it meant that, like Aunt Mani, my mother was free at last. Finally at peace. Perhaps it meant that I was free of her at last but the years to come would belie this. Ten years, not until I returned for my second India trip and, at thirty-two, finally started growing up. Ten years of grief.

REINVENTIONS

1

SUNDAY, JANUARY 22, 1978. Joga-Rao dropped me at my grandmother's house to bathe and change. Meanwhile, he cancelled his train reservations to Vizag. He could receive his distinguished alumnus award some other time. The bath was such a relief; so was the ointment, made from coconut oil, which softened my skin. Then I returned to his house. There I found a new tin of kerosene that someone had left outside the back door. I carried it into the back room and placed it under the washstand.

Ramumama was in the front room. He'd been one of my mother's dearest friends when I'd lived in India as a boy. My grandmother's call, the previous evening, had shaken him. He'd sent two of his friends – the couple who had visited while I'd sat on the front step – to see to Rukmini and my cousins. He sat now on the verge of tears while we spoke. As though apologizing, he said, "You see none of us expected it." He folded back his sleeve and showed me a burn on his forearm. The burn was almost healed into a welt. "I felt such pain," he said. "God knows what she endured." He seemed about to say more but two of my cousins entered. He and I rose and went outside. We drifted away from the house, toward the gate. There I asked him what rituals I should observe. I knew little about such things.

"At the very least, you should have the ashes immersed at Srirangapatna," he said. "There is a holy place there." He also said that normally I should hold a *mahapuja*, a great *puja* or ceremony, on the day my mother's soul enters heaven, but he suggested an alternative: a poor feeding, a feeding of the poor. (We did the latter a year later, though I wasn't there, on the first anniversary of her death, at a Bangalore charity).

I agreed because it all seemed so practical.

Mid-morning found us at Victoria Hospital, Joga-Rao, his three colleagues and I. We'd been driven there in a car from the Institute. The post-mortem section – the morgue – was a long building somewhat removed from the hospital. Access to the courtyard was through a locked gate guarded by a policeman. We waited in the courtyard, which was more like a small garden, and watched the entrance to the morgue itself. It was like the entrance to a prison, guarded by a door of iron bars. Even the veranda running the length of the building was faced with iron bars. Joga-Rao and I sat on stone benches at a round stone table sheltered by a tree. Suba-Rao and Nanjan-Rao spoke among themselves at a distance. Raja paced.

Outside, beyond the high walls, I could hear the constant noise of traffic. I, too, began pacing. Then I heard a crow. It had landed in the tree near the stone table, the one at which Joga-Rao sat. When a whitish-green blob fell on his head, he barely moved. I pretended not to notice – either what had happened or his slowness to react – and he said nothing. He merely took a handkerchief from his pocket and wiped at his hair. But the more he wiped, the more diluted the mess became and the farther it spread. It never occurred to me to take the kerchief from him and offer to help. It never occurred to him to ask.

"The ruby bangles she was wearing?" he told me after a while. "You may not get them back."

I understood, but I didn't care. The sub-inspector and the policeman had tried to remove them for us the evening before, but my mother's wrists had been too swollen.

"They must be worth five thousand at least," Joga-Rao said. He meant in rupees; over five hundred dollars.

"These things happen," Raja told me. Then, to Joga-Rao: "I shall go finish the arrangements."

I have two versions of what happened next, between the time Raja left us in the courtyard and the time we reached the crematorium. One version is from the notes I made two weeks later, in February 1978. The second is from my reconstruction – from memory – of these events. That was twelve years later, in June 1990. That was before I thought to go looking for the notes. It's not that I'd lost them; I'd simply forgotten they existed. I found them, written with a fountain pen on grey foolscap, folded into the back of a pink Hilroy exercise book.

According to the notes:

To everyone's surprise, my mother's jewellery was returned intact. The bangles and necklace would have to be kept in Joga-Rao's house until the police were disposed to release them to me. Next, we went to a crowded, dirty market across the street. Here we bought bamboo matting, cloth for a shroud, twine, and eau de cologne. I was once more fascinated by the sight of women and children seemingly camped under an arcade. Also by two half-naked infants fighting over a toy: a cardboard box top. Back at the post-mortem building, we waited while the body was wrapped.

The black corporation van arrived. It had glass sides and a glass back and two benches — one for the body and another for male mourners. Then the body was brought out. To my chagrin, the face had been left exposed. I desperately wanted to be spared the effort of riding in the van and, to my relief, two men whom the registrar had summoned from the Institute acted as mourners. After suitable tips were dispensed, we left for Wilson Gardens.

But according to my vivid reconstruction of these events, I never went to the market, and there was no corporation van:

Raja left us in the courtyard. "He is finding us a taxi," Joga-Rao said, "He will also buy a mat to wrap the body. And some cologne for the smell."
We waited. Each time the morgue door opened and clanged shut, Joga-Rao turned to look at it. Then he returned to watching the ground. Just as he had the day before, he sat with his shoulders hunched and his clasped hands between his knees. While I paced, he smoked.
Raja returned. "They have released the body," he announced. I looked at the barred door but saw nothing. He clearly had his ways.
Outside, Joga-Rao and I found the taxi waiting. A body wrapped in a mat lay tied on top. Joga-Rao and I took our places in the back. Nanjan-Rao and Suba-Rao climbed into the Institute car, then Raja took his place on the front seat of the taxi. Even as we set off, he handed a small packet back to me. Inside were a gold chain and, cut and bent, two ruby bangles.
"How?" I asked.
Joga-Rao shook his head. "I never expected to see these again," he said. "You are very fortunate." Then: "You will

have to leave these in my house until the police are disposed to release them to you."

"That should not take long," Raja said from the front. "Of
course we are still making a few payments."

"How much so far?" I asked.

"Not much," he said. "Two hundred, two-fifty."

When I tried to thank Joga-Rao, he looked out the window. His hand turned slightly on his thigh.

⟶⁑⟵

AT WILSON GARDENS we pulled up behind another vehicle and
got out. Attendants lowered the body from the top of our taxi
(or took it out of the van). Either way, I looked elsewhere.

Joga-Rao pointed out the mourners brought by Nanjan-
Rao from the Institute. The man who stood closest to the
body looked puzzled. "He was there when your mother was
finishing her PhD," Joga-Rao said. That would have been fifteen years ago. "He is likely trying to recognize her."

A curious onlooker – a tall, husky man with an unpleas-
ant face and a large moustache – approached my mother's
body. "Was it an accident?" he asked.

"Yes," Nanjan-Rao said sternly. "An accident."

The body ahead of ours was that of an aged scholar. His
family had arranged for special rites and so, at the side of the
crematorium, two priests performed a ceremony. It seemed
to have little meaning for the relatives. The priests had to
tell them where to stand and what to do and even, sometimes, to instruct one another. It was like watching a rehearsal: a dress rehearsal for mourning. After attendants
carried the scholar's body into the building, the priests
squatted in a circle at some distance from a small mound of
rice. It had been used in the ceremony. While one of the
scholar's relatives dropped coins to the priests, a girl who

had been watching – a street girl or urchin – crept forward and stole the rice. Then, while the relatives entered the crematorium, still another hanger-on, this one with his face smeared with ashes and a large red-orange spot on his forehead, begged for alms with an idiotic grin. No one tried to shoo him away.

It all seemed quite normal: that so much would go on at one time here; that neither hunger nor idiocy could pause for death.

Joga-Rao and I waited our turn with Raja on a small balcony. We would enter from here. Occasionally Nanjan-Rao and Suba-Rao joined us on the balcony. Raja had been a petty officer in the navy; the other men listened to his anecdotes; then all four men traded anecdotes about other deaths. What more could they do? I watched the two priests. They were having their heads shaved before entering the baths. At last we entered the crematorium itself.

My mother's body lay on a bamboo frame lashed with twine. The frame rested on a low metal trolley near huge doors. The trolley stood on rails that led toward the furnace doors. Near the doors were piled more bamboo frames. At last an attendant cranked open the doors and we could see flames inside the furnace. A second attendant pushed the trolley forward. When the front wheels reached the doors, the back of the trolley tilted up. My mother's body, wrapped in its matting and lashed to the bamboo, slid feet first into the furnace. The matting caught fire. The attendant pulled back the now empty trolley. Even as the first attendant cranked the huge doors shut, the bamboo frame ignited.

"We will come back tomorrow for the ashes," Joga-Rao said. "Now let us take lunch."

We did: a light lunch, in a well-appointed restaurant nearby, on Double Road. I was in such a fog, I have no memory of what we ate. Then we returned in the Institute car to

233

Joga-Rao's house just as an autorickshaw was leaving.

My father stood speaking with my Aunt Rukmini in the doorway of the house. He came out to the gate. Even as I got out of the car, he asked, "Are you all right, Boy?"

"Yes," I replied. Of course I was all right. I was surprised that he'd come all this way – from Debur Road to Nanjangud, from Nanjangud to Mysore, and from Mysore to Bangalore – but I said nothing.

Joga-Rao introduced him to the three men. I had no idea how to thank them – the three who had ensured everything would go smoothly. While I followed Joga-Rao and my father to the house, they left in the Institute car.

"Your Mrs. Rukmini is a bit upset," my father told Joga-Rao.

Yes, she was. She still broke into tears from time to time while the four of us sat talking in the front room. My father also looked tired and upset. He spoke in short sentences when he spoke at all. Later, Rukmini called in my cousins and he tried to be merry with them. He left before supper. He had to return to the house on Debur Road because he had to be at work the next day.

After supper, while the girls helped Rukmini clear the table, I tried to wash my mother's gold chain but the links were too charred to come clean. I put the chain back with the ruby bangles, now in Joga-Rao's care. Then I played French cricket with my cousin Sinu. We played behind the house. We played almost as though nothing unusual had happened – almost, because we were careful to avoid a patch of sand just outside the back door. If the ball rolled anywhere near the darkened sand, we stepped carefully around it. The evening before, it had been a pool of blood.

Two days later, I took the steam train to Mysore City and the diesel train to Nanjangud. In the cloth bag on my lap was an earthenware pot holding my mother's ashes. I'd looked inside only once, after receiving it from the crematorium. Poking from the yellow-grey ash had been part of a vertebrate. I hadn't looked inside since. At Nanjangud Railway Station, I hired a *jetka* – a horse-drawn cart – to take me to our house on Debur Road. My legs had begun to ache because the skin behind my knees and around my ankles hadn't completely healed. Back in my room again, I stored the pot on a shelf to await the day of the immersion.

2

ON WEDNESDAY, FEBRUARY 1, ten days after the cremation, my father and I set out by taxi. First we went to Mysore to see Dr. Shankar. My skin condition was on the mend by now, and I have no recollection of our visit. Then we went eight kilometers farther north toward the town of Srirangapatna, which was once an island fortress. Our destination was some distance from the town, to a branch of the Kaveri River, known as a holy place. The stream wound into sight and passed away again under a stone causeway. On either side, broad steps covered the banks. Here some men bathed and some children played. On the opposite bank a boy spun thread on a long stick that ended in a top. This he spun against a leg while he pulled fibres of cotton from a sheaf under his arm. He walked about while he worked. Another boy, seated, wove a mat from reeds he picked from the water's edge. Next to the steps grew a huge tree. Stone slabs ringed its base – slabs carved with entwined *nagas*, cobras. I sat down on the rough, granite steps of the *ghat*, the immersion path leading to the river.

My father had suggested that I not immerse the ashes because he didn't want me taking chances with my skin. I agreed, surprised because he normally had little patience with Hindu rituals. He stripped to blue bathing trunks and cautiously edged onto a granite shelf where the murky, green water was knee-deep. He returned to sit with his legs in the water while a priest instructed him in the upcoming ritual, The light scum on the water's surface lapped at my father's legs. The pot stood at my feet. He picked it up and followed the priest out into the river.

I don't remember the order of the ritual. My father had to slip a ring knotted from a reed onto one of his fingers. He also had to slip on two Brahmin threads over his shoulders and across his heart – something he hadn't done since his wedding over twenty years before. The priest muttered verses and sometimes asked my father to repeat them with his hands clasped below his chin. The only phrase I made out was "*Lakshmi devi.*" It meant Goddess Lakshmi, the goddess for whom my mother was named. Then he had to sip water from the river. First, though, he carefully parted the light scum on the surface to find water that was clear if not clean.

Meanwhile, oblivious to this ritual, a second priest circled the huge tree and did homage to gods who lingered nearby. Men bathed and children played. A boy spun thread. Another boy wove a mat. So much went on at one time, and few things could pause for death.

Again, I have two versions of what happened next. In my reconstruction of twelve years later:

> Finally the priest nodded. My father took the pot from the bottom step and lowered it into the water. The lid floated free, and the pot bubbled air on its way down. I remember the day was bright. The taxi had waited and we set off home. The red earth of southern Mysore looked richer than usual, and there was a wind in the trees. It was a long drive back, but my father said little. Neither of us had spo-

ken about what had happened. Finally he said, "If only she had given India a chance." It was the only thing he would ever say about my mother's death.

But I found this in my notes, made a week after the immersion:

> Finally the priest nodded. My father poured river water into the pot. Standing with his back to the stream, he threw the pot back, high, over his head. The pot landed in mid-stream and sank at once. "Don't look back," the priest warned. The only remark my father had made in the ten days since the cremation was this one, on our way to the holy place near Srirangapatna:

> "It would have been easy for your mother to live in India. It's too bad she couldn't look a little bit ahead."

As far as I could tell, there was only one immediate effect of my mother's death. It was an effect I hoped would pass, and it did pass: a fear of losing my father. This happened if he became ill with the flu or his heart bothered him. My dream was to bring him back to Canada to live near or with me once more. But this feeling, too, passed. Over the years we became as estranged as we'd become during my teens.

In March, 1978, on my way back to Canada, I stopped in Hyderabad to visit my Aunt Sita. Her husband was my other maternal uncle, Amba-Rao, the rocket scientist. They were not estranged and were, in fact, still very much a couple; but while his work took him to various American cities, Sita sometimes lived in India. I knew her fairly well from my several visits to them. I hadn't seen her in nearly ten years, not since a family gathering in New Brunswick, New Jersey, and yet we spoke with ease. She was the only person of her generation – she was the youngest of all my aunts and uncles, just fifteen years older than me – with whom I felt I could have a proper dialogue. With the others, I had monologues – they spoke and I listened. She seemed to understand there was no value in enduring life's difficulties with false strength. And I would realize, some years later, that I'd endured my mother's death with a numbness bordering on exactly this: a false strength. I'd taken part in everything, watched and listened, but said little. I hadn't moved as if in a daze; I'd simply moved. Sita also seemed to be the only person who could say more than, "I am sorry to hear about your mother." That's what others did – all of them. Then again, I would later wonder what more they could have said; think that there's no shame at being at a loss for words.

On my second afternoon in Hyderabad, Sita and I had our coffee on the terrace of her flat. She wore a yellow blouse and a white sari with a yellow border. Bougainvillea grew nearby. The terrace overlooked the low hills of Hyderabad, and we laughed over the tour bus at a nearby house, which belonged to a movie star. Tour buses regularly stopped at his gate so that people could claim they had seen his house. Even take photographs.

At last Sita said something very like what I'd imagined my father had said until I found my notes. But she didn't say, "If only she had given India a chance." Instead Sita said, "If only she had given us a chance. We could have helped her." Then she asked me how I felt: asked me in a way that invited an honest reply.

"I couldn't tell the others," I said, "but it almost feels like a relief."

"How?" she asked, neither surprised nor, I could see, ready to pass judgment on me.

"I saw it coming," I said. "I've known for ten years now that she would die. It was the timing that surprised me." Either Sita assumed I was still in shock or, more likely, she understood. I think she understood. For so long, until it no longer mattered, I so desperately wanted them all to understand – until, finally, I saw that they never would.

One last thing: how good we are at forgetting; how good we are at inducing amnesia.

Each year, as January 21st neared, I forgot the significance of that day. The next day or the next, I once again remembered. It was a game I played every year for ten years after that first India trip. Then, on January 21, 1989, after my second India trip – the one I never wanted to make but finally did – I allowed myself to remember: "This is the day my mother killed herself." It wasn't the end of anything. It was another beginning. However much I would like it all to end here, it won't end. I went back after all, though I'd promised myself I never would. I went back with my Canadian-born fiancee although I wanted to protect her from all of this. I learned she wasn't the one who needed protecting and I learned more:

Something has to follow amnesia – if not memory, then reinvention.

Epilogue

TAMPERING

BEGAMUDRE MEANS LOCKSEAL. The first of our clan works in a royal treasury. Each night he locks it, sews a cloth around the lock, and stamps the royal seal onto wax. Next morning, if he finds the seals broken, he will know that someone has broken in.

My grandfather begins life as Beegamudre Nelawanki Krishna-Rao, Nelawanki the name of his father's village. After his father loses his land, my grandfather changes his family name to Begamudre, which is shortened as B. Krishna-Rao. Thus, he becomes a man with no land to his name.

He names my father Rakosh, formally B. Rakosh-Das, after a Hungarian Freemason named Rakoczi. His mother calls him Rakosh or, when impatent, Rakosh-Das. She names her favourite son Ananda. This means happiness or joy.

When my mother is pregnant (with me) she prays to Lord Venkateswara for a son, promises to name him after the Lord. I am born B. Venkateswara, sometimes Venkatesh.

Ashbury College, Ottawa, day one. Mrs. Dalton is taking roll. When she asks for my family name, I give it. When she asks for my given name, I give her that too. She takes both my names and gives me back Venkatesh Begamudre. At once I have been reborn and christened.

We use only last names at Ashbury. Brothers pose no problem. We have a Luciano One and a Luciano Two. Classmates find Begamudre too long. To them I become V.B. Who am I to deny them the comfort of abbreviations? This is their land.

240

My mother's parents named her Lakshmi, formally Lakshmi-Bai, after the goddess of wealth. My father calls her Lakshmi-Bai She calls him sir.

He cringes when she calls me Babu, "Boy" in her mother tongue. He thinks the name too soft. He thinks me too soft. He calls me either V.B. or Boy. His hand, when it strikes, is not soft.

Because my father and I have different last names, people ask if I am adopted. Sometimes I wonder too. He will later reverse his name to match mine. By then it will no longer matter (to me) whose son I am.

Mrs. Going ("Call me Granny") is my first babysitter. She thinks my given name, now also my first, is Venkatish. Shortens it to Tish. That's what people later call me in Kingston. That and, "Tissue, I need you, achoo!"

"Reach for the Top", Vancouver, first night of taping. A technician finds Venkatesh too long for the acrylic sign he fabricates. He shortens it to Ven. Thank you, Lord.

Some people hear it as Ben. Others ask, "As in Venn diagram?" Friends reply, "As in vending machine," and I pretend amusement. Two men, scholars and gentlemen, say *min vän* means my friend in Swedish. I consider moving.

Schiller College, Paris, day one. The principal keeps dropping the last *e* in Begamudre. When I say it's pronounced like an *a*, she adds an accent *aigu*. People appear bemused especially because, thanks to a professor named J.J. Van Vlasselaer, I speak French with a Belgian accent.

Back in India now, my cousins try hard to call me Ven. I wish they wouldn't. I wish I were the same Venkatesh who left as a boy. Someone has been in the treasury. We know because the seals are cracked. The lock has not been forced, but even a cursory inspection reveals tampering.

Saskatoon, Canada, Summer 1983
Regina, Canada, Summer 2017

BONUS MATERIALS

A calendar picture of Raghavendra Swami

Gandhi Himself

An Unfinished Story

Raja loved Padmini more than he loved his own wife; even more than he loved his seven children and fifteen grandchildren – excepting, perhaps, the first grandson. Yet Padmini was neither a concubine nor a temple dancer. Scoff if you must: Padmini was his motorcar. Strictly speaking, she belonged to the government depot but one would have risked his present life and the next by suggesting that Raja had no right to call her his. He had, after all, been her first driver. Perhaps not the very first, but nearly enough. He ignored the unworthy who had driven her from the docks of Madras to the receiving depot in Mysore. And by assuming that she had been built next to the sea, then gently lifted on board a ship, he completely begged the question of whether she had allowed any foreigners in Michigan, America, inside her. Let no one doubt it: this Ford Model T, born in 1927, was his alone. During their five years together, he had calmed her nerves through every change of lubricant and spark plug and nursed her through shattered windscreens. He had even christened her by painting *MC Padmini* on the back of her sun visor. When he flipped it down, which he did even on cloudy days, she proudly told passengers her name. *MC* stood for His Majesty's Conveyance. Yet he was no mere village-bred lout wise with native cunning. Not our Raja. He fully understood his passion for her, and so he wavered between exhilaration and dread over his newest assignment, if only because he had not received it in the usual manner.

His supervisor, Nari, had not called Raja into his cramped office. Nari had not flourished a requisition signed by some government officer or his secretary. Most strange of all, Nari had not dictated an itinerary. None of these. Nari had actually come running to where Raja had been sitting in the compound near Padmini and demanded, "Did you see Him?" The manner in which he had said *Him* suggested that he meant Vishnu or Shiva; perhaps Brahma himself.

"I have heard more hymns than I have seen," Raja had said. "My auntie is a Christian."

Nari had neither laughed nor snickered, for he did so at only his own jests.

"I saw him," Raja had said. "What is there to cackle about?" His flippancy had belied the intrigue he had felt upon glimpsing Him through the grimy window of Nari's office. Him had not spent the usual half hour Nari kept officers waiting while he decided which motorcar to assign. Nor had Him craned, undignified, over Nari's desk while signing the receipt. Him had merely produced a letter from the pocket of his high-necked suit jacket, passed it to Nari, and taken it back. Him had then left. Raja suspected Him to be a senior-most officer, yet Him could not have been a day over forty, a youngster to someone like Raja. Fully fifty-one years of age, he faced only four years of active service before he could retire with full pension. "So what is there?" he repeated.

"He," replied Nari with the same reverence accorded to Him, "asked for number twelve." This was Padmini's proper designation, yet Raja never used it. Let the other drivers call their motorcars by number. Would a ship steer straight or a temple dancer lie still if one coaxed, however gently, "Steady, number twelve"?

"By name?" Raja asked.

"Of course not, madcap!" Nari scoffed. "He requested the most plain motorcar we have."

"And you gave him Padmini?"

"He also wanted the roadworthiest motorcar in our depot," Nari explained. "That is number...is your motorcar, correct?"

"Of course correct." Raja agreed guardedly, for he had not dared report Padmini's most recent ailment: an occasionally blocked petrol line. Nari would order him to surrender her to the government repair depot, whose louts manhandled everything from railway ticket punches to dented steam-rollers. God only knew what indignities she might suffer there: unwrapped coils, likely; or, worse, stripped bolts.

"So, Maharaj," Nari asked expansively. "Guess where you are both off to?"

"Ayodhya?" Raja asked. "America to see the Vizier of Oz?"

Nari actually laughed. He shouted, "You are to drive Him to see the Diwan himself!"

Raja's eyes opened wider than an owl's on a moonless night, wider even than the gulf bridged by Hanuman's mon-key soldiers to invade Lanka.

Nari looked suddenly nervous over having attracted cu-rious frowns from other drivers. "He bore a letter signed by the Diwan himself," he explained. "The chief minister, I tell you!" He screwed up his eyes, more for effect than for aid, while recalling the words: "The bearer, Sri G. Mohandas, is entitled to any or all assistance he may request in the course of his duties, such assistance to be rendered without ques-tion. God save the King-Emperor! It was signed by the Diwan himself," Nari repeated. "Have I not with these very two eyes seen his signature enough times to–?"

"Gopal Mohandas?" someone exclaimed.

Raja frowned up to see Mola, the juniormost driver, standing with one hand on Padmini's bonnet. He removed his hand when Raja scowled. "Has Mr. Mohandas been transferred here?" Mola asked. "When did he come?"

"When you were sleeping in the back of number five," Nari replied.

"And you did not waken me?" Mola's eyes darted about the walled compound as though he expected Him to reappear. The junior driver looked stricken but he grew animated while he explained, "I drove for him last year only. Such a great man!"

"But who is He?" Nari hissed.

Mola also squatted. He dabbled the pool of oil with his toes, their thick nails uncut. "Only the most honest engineer in South India!" he declared. "Mr. Mohandas reports to the Diwan himself!"

"We know that," Raja scoffed. "The letter–"

"He bore a letter last year also," Mola said, "when I drove him down to Ooty. Only then he was stationed at Chickmagalur. The Diwan must want him closer at hand." Mola stared between Raja and Nari as though at a vision. "Such a great man," he repeated, yet he spoke without inflating his tones as Nari had. Mola also spoke with a familiarity lacking one syllable of contempt, as Raja often did of his own passengers. "Even in my next life, I shall not forget him," Mola said. "I drove him to the Ooty dam site. It was being built then only and he went up into the hillside, never mind the snakes. I helped him to count how many baskets of earth how many coolies carried in how many quarter hours. He had a fine pocket watch he could stop and make go."

"Why all this 'how many?'" Nari demanded.

"Listen, I am telling you," Mola exclaimed. "The Diwan suspected the contractors of reporting lies. Of saying this much earth had been dug when only this much had been dug For each *this much* Mola held his hands far apart, then close together as though manipulating some foreign instrument. A concertina. "The longer we remained at the dam site, the more questions Mr. Mohandas put to the head contractor."

"That is also whom I would put them to," Raja said.

"Ho!" Mola exclaimed. "When have you dared to address an Angrez?"

Raja's scowl at Mola's impudence went unnoticed. "This head contractor was one Mr. Jonathan Welltrap," Mola explained. "He was known by all the chief engineers in South India. When I questioned Mr. Mohandas later on why he bothered Mr. Welltrap, he said to me that if the contractors cheated the government, then Mr. Welltrap must be helping. That night we slept in Ooty because Mr. Welltrap would not offer a cot in the camp. Mr. Mohandas does not sleep on floors. "Next morning I once again drove him to the dam site. Some goonda had left a lorry sideways on the town side of the bridge. A factory-new lorry, a Bedford. We could see Mr. Welltrap in front of the site office. He was surrounded by his foremen. His foremen surrounded him. Rough looking goondas, all of them, but Mr. Mohandas began crossing the bridge. What to do? Of course I ran, calling him back, for I feared those foremen would break his thirty-two teeth. But Mr. Welltrap signalled to his foremen to go up the hillside. All the coolies were dropping their tools. Here each coolie was earning fifty *paise* each day for taking out this much earth only and earning twice, thrice that for the cheaters, who said each man took out this much earth."

"You are practising to play at a wedding?" Nari asked. He smiled disdainfully at the invisible concertina.

Mola continued: "When the coolies began running down the hillside, I feared they had been ordered by the foremen to beat us both. But, no, the coolies ran through the camp laughing like children. The foremen could not keep them back, lathis, no lathis. Mr. Mohandas and Mr. Welltrap met in the middle of the bridge. It fell so quiet, I thought the bridge had collapsed from all the coolies gathering now behind Mr. Welltrap. I thought Yama himself would ride past any moment on his buffalo, fix his copper eyes on me, lick his green lips, and drag me off to hell. But I saw Mr. Welltrap point his swaggering stick at Mr. Mohandas. I heard Mr. Welltrap enquire, "What is it you want here?"

"Mr. Mohandas said, 'I have come to examine your accounting books. Only then may I write my report.'"

"Mr. Welltrap said, 'Mr. Mohandas, if you submit your report, I shall ensure you are broken so low you will spend the rest of your service digging latrines!'"

"And Mr. Mohandas said, 'Mr. Welltrap, if I am broken that low, I shall ensure you will spend the rest of your service cleaning those latrines.'"

Mola clasped his hands in front of his shins and sighed. His lips curved in a smile so peaceful that it might have been induced by toddy. His eyes roiled back under his fluttering eyelids. He looked as though he had been driver to the Viceroy himself.

"What happened then?" Raja demanded. He flicked an oily rag at Mola's fly "Tell us, you udderless cow."

Mola frowned as though the end should have been clear. "The coolies laughed. Every last man of them. Mr. Welltrap's face turned red as Kali's tongue. He beat his way like this, like that through the crowd. He shouted at the foremen to get everyone back to work, but even the foremen disobeyed. They did not benefit so much from the cheating, after all. Only some little *baksheesh*. One brought a table. Another brought a chair. Right in the middle of the bridge, Mr. Mohandas sat down to question the coolies. They told how much earth they took away each week and how much they earned. This enquiry lasted the entire day. I fetched Mr. Mohandas his hotel food for lunch and supper from Ooty itself. No cold tiffin-carrier food for him! The *sambar* was as hot when he drank it as when I left the town, I drove that fast." Mola shrugged as though ending a tale about a youthful tryst. "Then we left. Even though he could not examine the accounting books, only the accounting Mr. Welltrap sent to the district engineer, Mr. Mohandas made his report. Less than two-thirds of the earth had been removed only. All the contractors were thrown into jail."

"And your Mr. Welltrap?" Nari asked.

Mola blew his nose and wiped his wet fingers on the ground. He rolled a ball of sticky dust between his fingers, then flicked it well away from Padmini. "Mr. Jonathan Welltrap is Angrez. He works in some other state now."

"So," Nari exclaimed. "I wonder where you are off to with this most honest officer?" His knees cracked when he rose.

Leaving Mola to himself, Raja also rose, but his knees did not crack. "You have the memory of an elephant!" he snapped. "I am driving him to see the Diwan."

Nari grinned with the delight of a superior who has withheld some crucial bit of information. "He intimated that was his first stop only," Nari said. "Did I forget to tell you that? So sorry, Maharaj. He would not tell even me, an officer almost, where you are driving him to for one entire week."

"He is on another mission!" Mola cried. He leapt to his feet and clutched Raja's forearm. "You be certain to say *namaskaara* for me! You be certain to say, 'Mola the Driver enquires after the children.'"

Raja nodded. Later, he nodded to himself, alone. He polished a final cloud from the sheen on Padmini's front left wing. It had been dented in a crash with a bullock cart. Only the fury of the bullock had prevented him from soundly thrashing the villager on the cart. Moreover, half the load of green coconuts, heavy with their cooling milk, had fallen on the fellow. Raja would have had to dig him out. He scowled at the other motorcars. They were lined up on two sides of the compound while their drivers lounged in the shade. They smoked *beedis* the whole day long while waiting for assignments. Some of the motorcars had holders bolted on their front wings to take the little flags flown when conveying a government minister. Padmini had never been fancy enough, like some of these newer Model A's, to warrant such recognition. True, her radiator shell had lost much of its nickel plating. Still and all, she would have looked grand with her horn blaring and flags flying even if she would not be photographed for some illustrated magazine; even if she would bear only a district engineer on some secret mission. Raja enjoyed secrets, especially revealing them. He only hoped that this sudden departure would not tax Padmini. He wanted no young officer, full of his own self-importance, to treat her like a mere motorcar. Let no one doubt it: Padmini was a goddess.

TWO HOURS LATER Raja reported for duty. It might have been three, since he had secretly pawned his government-issued Railway timepiece. Mr. Mohandas's house was not only smaller than Raja had envisioned but it was also in an odd location for one as obviously well salaried as an engineer. It stood a furlong off Madhvacharya Road and within sight of the Government Sandalwood Factory. The sweet fumes of sandalwood reducing to oil made the air as foul as the smoke blanketing cremation grounds.

Raja switched off Padmini's motor. He climbed out to find two boys eyeing him from behind a low, wrought-iron gate. The elder, perhaps ten, held a red leather ball and a new cricket bat. It glistened with linseed oil. The younger, by perhaps two years, wore black-rimmed spectacles. "Mr. Mohandas lives here?" Raja asked.

The cricket player nodded. While the brother continued staring at Padmini, Raja realized what was wrong with the boy's eyes that he already needed spectacles: Nothing – they were made of clear glass. They seemed an expensive toy but Mohandas likely made *lakhs* of rupees; *crores*, perhaps. The elder boy ran to the verandah to call, "Appa, Driver is here!"

A girl of twelve or thirteen, barely old enough for the new sari she wore, appeared in the verandah with a brown cardboard suitcase and a bedroll. Raja opened the gate to fetch the shabby luggage. He turned with the suitcase hefted onto his left shoulder and the bedroll tucked under his left arm. The younger boy stood on Padmini's running board. Even with his fingers hooked over the open window, even stretched up onto his tiptoes, the boy could not reach her controls. As quickly as Raja's protectiveness re-appeared, it vanished in the blast of a voice from behind:

"Nagasha!"

The spectacled boy turned and so did Raja. Uneasiness welled up from his bowels like gas from a stale poppadom, for he had seen the man in the verandah before. True, he was the same mysterious Mohandas whom Raja had glimpsed through the window of Nari's office. Still, Raja felt he knew Mohandas's face intimately. It was a face Raja recalled from his earlier days of repairing motorcycles and motorcars, his days of driving Bedford buses with sagging springs from Tirumala Link Station up the hill to the temple of Lord Venkateswara. Yet that in itself was impossible. Had he known Mohandas so long ago, his face would surely have aged and yet...and yet it was the same. His greying, dark hair had been cropped close to the skull by some enthusiastic barber, and his ears stuck out like those of an elephant. Most disturbing of all, however, were those round, wire-rimmed spectacles perched on the bridge of a broad nose, one so long that its tip sagged in front of an almost grey moustache. Some strange force, certainly not awe of officers, compelled Raja to place the bedroll atop the now lowered suitcase. He joined his palms in front of his breast and greeted, "*Namaskaara*, sir."

"Let us be off," Mohandas said. His speech was as clipped as his hair.

"Of course, sir!" Raja exclaimed. Once again he picked up the luggage.

The younger boy stood with his arms outstretched to Mohandas. No farewell hug, no pat on the head. None of these. "Get down now," he said. "Join your brother."

The boy made a great show of dragging his feet through the dust back to the gate. The elder brother still clutched his cricket bat and ball. The sister rearranged her sari over her shoulder. It looked all skin and bones, that shoulder.

Raja opened the rear door for Mohandas. He climbed into Padmini without so much as a farewell, not even a nod, to his children. Raja climbed in behind Padmini's steering column and started her motor. A movement in the corner of his eye, a movement like the blur of a wasp, made him turn his head. He saw a woman: Mohandas's wife, very likely; the mother of his children. She stood on the verandah step and her mouth was pinched.

"What are you waiting for?" Mohandas demanded.

For the woman to wave as the children now did, sadly. "Nothing, sir," Raja said. "Not a one." In his haste he nearly stripped Padmini's gears. With forced cheer he called, "Next stop, Diwan's office!"

Several, silent minutes later, he halted Padmini in front of the new government building, around the corner from the Maharajah's palace. Mohandas tapped Raja's shoulder with a one-rupee note. *Baksheesh* already? A bribe? Dumbfounded, Raja awkwardly caught the note. "Not necessary, sir," he said.

"Yes, it is," Mohandas insisted. He climbed out. "I shall be a few minutes only, fifteen at most. You go to the bazaar and buy for me a dhoti and body cloth. Also a shawl for the nighttime."

"A disguise, sir?" Raja asked.

"Do it now, driver," Mohandas said. He turned to acknowledge the sentry's salute with a nod, one as curt as the order.

Ho, Raja, Maharaj, shopping for goods with an entire rupee! For that much he could buy the finest cloth in Mysore. Yet his thriftiness led him to a stall in Devaraja Market rather than to one of the shirtings shops near the palace. He picked over a bolt of Lancashire cotton, one of many stacked on a table that filled most of the stall. He told the vendor how much material was required.

"Twelve *annas* for plenty cotton," the vendor said.

"For twelve *annas*," Raja scoffed, "I can clothe my entire family, hangers-on to boot, and have enough to wipe your nose, you son of a fermented horse dropping!"

He pointed at a single bolt of coarse, poorly-bleached cotton lying under the table. "How much?" he demanded.

"Six *annas*," the vendor said, scowling. "It is *khaddar* only."

Raja returned to the government building to find Mohandas smoking in the open verandah. Raja expected Mohandas would smoke Angrez cigarettes – tailor-made Players Navy Cut, perhaps – but no. Even as Mohandas approached, Raja smelled the familiar acrid tobacco of a *beedi*. Thus, he felt no surprise when Mohandas asked for both the cloth and his change. Clearly the man was no spendthrift. Raja handed the folded cloth back, then dropped the two coins into the waiting palm.

"Do they call this cotton?" Mohandas demanded. He began plucking at nubs of twisted thread. He gave up after tossing a few out his open window.

"*Khaddar* only," Raja said. "Why, Mahatma Gandhi himself might have spun it at his ashram! Homespun in his very home!"

"I spend all my earnings to ensure my nephews and nieces do not have to grow up village louts," Mohandas scoffed, "and this Mahatma wants to turn India into one giant village?"

"You are not from Mysore, sir?" Raja asked.

"Nelawanki," came the reply. "Kolar District."

Raja nodded with understanding. The Nelawanki Gopals were notorious for their orthodoxy. No wonder Mohandas had such high principles. He smoked, however. Raja frowned at the name of his motorcar painted so lovingly on the sun visor. Names told much, yes. "And your father, sir?" he asked. "What is he? Schoolmaster? Collector, even?" The sudden flare of a match set the hairs on the back of his neck to prickle. The next instant, smoke streamed past his left shoulder.

"My father," Mohandas said at last, "was a fool. He believed simplicity was good for both body and soul, just like this great soul of yours in beggars' clothing. This Mahatma."

Puzzling over these words, Raja tried to decide whether he liked Mohandas; whether he was the heroic figure Mola had thought him. Not since his youth had Raja heard anyone laugh about Gandhi. For Mohandas to act so coolly toward his wife – well, that was normal. But how could a man who acted so coolly toward his children be so forthright as to care about honesty? Perhaps, Raja thought, a man did not need to be compassionate to have principles. Raja's head began clouding with ideas. To clear it, he honked Padinini's horn at a cow.

"Slow down here," Mohandas ordered. Padmini had reached the point where Harishchandra Road neared the racecourse. "Turn right onto Sankara Road."

"We are beginning our mission, sir?"

"Not until we reach our destination. We are going to Ooty."

Raja gripped the wheel atop Padmini's steering column. The original metal wheel had cracked, so he had replaced it with a fine wooden one already stained with sweat from his forever-oily palms. "More dirty dealings, sir?" This time he kept the excitement from his voice when he said, "Mola the Driver says *namaskaara*. He enquires after the children."

Mohandas grunted. "I suppose he intimated the reason for my last journey to Ooty?" he asked.

Raja shrugged and said, "Little here, little there."

"Then I shall also intimate a little here, a little there," Mohandas said. "What you need to know, only. The superintending engineer there has asked our service to make an inspection of the Ooty Dam since he does not trust his own district engineers. We shall stay this night in Nanjangud town. Unfortunately, I am known to the Ooty power station manager, so I must disguise myself like some common criminal. It is terrible when an honest man must resort to such jiggery-pokery. Your Mola the Driver would look the same whatever he wore, so I could not chance his participation in this matter. You have some villagers' clothing?"

If by villagers' clothing Mohandas meant a dhoti and body cloth, yes, Raja had these in Padmini's boot. Still, he wondered whether Mohandas thought only city folk wore suit jackets, collared shirts, trousers and shoes. Raja frowned at his own ill-fitting khaki short pants and shirt. He had also been issued a pair of brown shoes but he preferred to drive barefoot. "What form of participation, sir?" he asked.

"You shall be my bearer and secretary," Mohandas said. His voice rose when he added, "People in my employ do not spit." Raja turned to see whether Mohandas was jesting about such a commonplace habit. "Keep both eyes on the road!" he ordered. "Neither do such people blow their noses with their fingers –"

"But I have no..." Raja began, then checked himself. "Yes, sir," he meekly said.

"You know how to write English?" Mohandas asked.

"No, sir," Raja replied. English was for the Angrez. And for people like Mohandas who fancied themselves Angrez. "Kannada only." At once, he cursed himself, for he could write nothing beyond his name.

"That is all right," Mohandas said. "I shall write my report based on your Kannada notes."

Raja's spirits sank below the patched coven of the front seat, below the coiled springs inside, almost as low as the suspension springs that flanked Padmini's wooden wheels. The road to Ooty did not promise to be smooth. Even the sight of the temple atop Chamundi Hill, now to Padmini's left, failed to revive his spirits. They fell even lower, into the potholes of Sankara Road, when Mohandas spoke again.

"Once we are at the dam site," he said, "we shall leave this motorcar and continue by local bus."

Raja shouted, "Leave Padmini!"

"Whom?" Mohandas asked.

"Leave my motorcar?" Raja demanded. His head swam with visions of the cruelty that strangers might inflict on her. Boys would climb onto her running boards, vendors would leave oily marks on her bonnet, dogs would make number one on her wheels. "It will be for a few days only," Mohandas said. This was not reassuring. "Three or four, at most."

Raja despaired. How could he leave Padmini defenceless in a strange place? She would never forgive him. As if she shared his visions of foreboding, she began conspiring against his plan of reaching Nanjangud by sunset. She had just passed the halfway point on the Mysore-Nanjangud Road, where it rejoined the railway track briefly before separating again, when her motor suddenly lost power. No bang from the pistons, no hiss from the radiator, no splintering crack from the wheels – none of these. Merely less power no matter how far Raja opened the throttle below the steering wheel. Finally, she stopped. He well suspected the cause of the problem. Still, he replied, "No problem, sir; not a one," after Mohandas demanded, "What is it now?"

Raja climbed out and lifted one side of Padmini's bonnet. He bent to avoid Mohandas's disgusted look. Raja unplugged her petrol line and began to suck out petrol. He spit out one mouthful, another, a third before clearing the obstruction. Had he not gagged and coughed, a clot of dirt would have slithered down his throat like a coiled, wet snake. Bending low, he spat to rid his mouth of the taste of petrol. He straightened, closed the bonnet, and patted it. "Behave now," he whispered. While he settled himself behind the steering column, he wiped his forearm across his lips. "You see, sir?" he mumbled. "Nothing to worry yourself about."

"Why then do I smell petrol?" Mohandas asked.

"What else does a motorcar run on, sir?" Raja asked. "Not

cow dung or coconut oil!" He forced himself to sound jovial when he asked, "Does a temple dancer not smell of rose water if she takes her head bath with –"

"I do not frequent TDs," Mohandas replied. Raja should have guessed this. The petrol smell could not have concerned Mohandas much, though, for he lit yet another *beedi* after Raja started Padmini's motor. She covered five miles before stopping once more. He unblocked the petrol line, then drove with his shoulders hunched. He expected to have his neck wrung at any moment. When the winding road began to slope down towards the valley of the Kabini River, he eased the strain on Padmini's petrol pump by shutting off her motor and allowing her to coast. She rolled more quickly than the lighter carts pulled by bullocks, yet not so quickly as the single government motorcycle that wove past her at an incredible forty miles per hour. Rather than peering into Padmini to see her passenger, the motorcyclist kept his goggled eyes turned away, and Raja wondered why a government messenger would ride so fast on such a winding road. Raja glared at the road bridge that led to Nanjangud. Padmini would have no trouble coasting the remaining way to the embankment but he did not fancy either having to repair her on the level bridge or having to push her across. Looking down to his right, he spied a ferry. "If we leave her here," he forced himself to suggest, "we can cross by that ferry, sir, and walk into the town. It will be more quick than following this road over the bridge." He hoped that Padmini was not listening. He had never abandoned her before now.

Mohandas leaned forward to scowl with Raja at the road. It stretched two furlongs east before turning south to cross the river. Mohandas ordered Raja to take the suitcase and bedroll from the boot. Also whatever effects, no doubt few, that Raja himself would require. Mohandas further ordered him to hold the ferry when it reached the near bank. Then Mohandas stepped behind a thick, gnarled banyan tree to change into his villagers' clothing.

"Why this jiggery-pokery so soon?" Raja asked.

"The local engineer is known to me," Mohandas replied. He folded his suit jacket. "We were all of us classmates, some junior, some senior." He placed it on a granite slab carved with an arrow and, Raja supposed, both the name of Nanjangud and the distance that remained. "He will suspect I am leaving my district for some purpose," Mohandas said. "He will alert all the districts nearby, even south of the state border. Such news, relayed quietly, spreads faster than news shouted from man to man. Leave the boot open so I may put my clothes inside. Why do you wait?"

With the suitcase, bedroll and his own bundle clasped atop his head, Raja followed the path down to the water. At times he skidded. He checked his hurtling progress by stamping his calloused heels into the mud. At times he simply ran. He leapt the larger stones, the plantain leaves, and even into and out of the discarded rubber tire of a lorry. Not once did his load fly loose. He kept his eyes on the ferry. It was the usual raft, this one made of old doors and poled by an old man bent to one side. It had reached midstream and was making for the near bank. Careful to unload his own bundle first, gently, Raja dumped Mohandas's suitcase and bedroll on a flat rock. Looking west, Raja marvelled at the low, reddening sun. The Kabini River reflected the sun as a blade in the quivering current. The sun even melted atop the water to the right and left in order to form a hilt. He saw not a sunset but a long, jagged, flaming sword.

Suddenly, a plump man appeared from behind a tamarind bush. He retied his dhoti while approaching Raja to await the ferry's arrival. Both men heard a branch snap, but the plump man turned first. Raja turned only when the man's eyes grew wide, wider even than the maw of a mewling infant. The man bowed over reverently clasped hands.

Raja felt a mischievous delight at the thought of someone's having already uncovered Mohandas's disguise. But when Raja looked up the path, he sucked in his breath. He whispered, "Rama-Krishna!" His one step backward sent him tumbling over the luggage. He fell off the rock and onto the river's very edge.

"Stop this foolishness!" Mohandas said, more to Raja than to the plump man. "Do I look like a ghost because I am dressed all in white?"

"N-no," Raja gurgled. He glanced at the man, whose eyes seemed never to blink. Mohandas looked like a real man all right; not a ghost. As real as any illusion could approach life. Except that the hair on his head was too dark, his calves below the dhoti's hem too muscular, and his bearing too erect – except for such minor details, he looked like the spitting image, identical twin, carbon copy of... Who could believe it? Mahatma Gandhi himself.

POSTCOLONIAL EULOGIES FOR THE
GRANDFATHER I NEVER MET

1. From the Bulletin of the Calcutta Mathematical Society, volume 40, 1948 (page 49):

> *Membership*: The Council learns with a deep sorrow of the death of Professor C. V. Hanumanta Rao, whose services as a former Vice-president and a member of the Board of Editors of the *Bulletin* the Council recalls with grateful appreciation.
>
> During the year under review four new members were elected.

2. From an article, "The Dual of a Theorem Proved by F. Morley, published by Henry Frederick Baker Cambridge, in a later number of volume 40, 1948 (page 226):

> I learn with deep regret, from the March number of the *Bulletin of the Calcutta Mathematical Society*, that my old and much respected friend, C.V. Hanumanta Rao, formerly Professor at Lahore, has died. So far as I know his last publications related to a theorem variously known by the names of Petersen, Hjemslev and Morley, taken to projective form. I should like

to offer the following lines for publication in tribute to my
late friend. They were actually written in correspondence
with him about his last two papers; and, as will be seen, the
result might appropriately be named for him.

In ordinary space of three dimensions, let u, v, w, u', v', w'
be six lines, passing through a point T, which lie on a
quadric cone. If we take any two ordered triads from these
lines, say u, v, w and u', v' and w', and consider the six
planes a=(v', w) a'=(v, w'), ß=(w', ß=(w, u') γ=(u', v), γ=(u,
v'), then the three lines of intersection of pairs of these (a,
a'), (ß, ß'), (γ, γ') lie in a plane through T...

3. From an interview with my Aunt Rama Menon in Vancouver, July 21, 1995, shortly before her 65th birthday:

Dates and places, I am not sure. It says in my diary — here it
is — Daddy was born 29th October, 1892. Does not say
when he died.

Nineteen forty-seven, yes. It must have been after 15th
August because we were independent.

No, Mommy's father was a civil engineer. Daddy's father
was a school inspector. You might ask Papalu, he knows
dates and places. He is like you, always asking what happened when.

Daddy caught tuberculosis in Lahore during the riots, the
Hindu-Muslim riots. He had grown a beard so people
would think he was Muslim and he would be safe. Then,
one day, he was sitting reading the newspaper in his hotel,
and a Hindu fellow tried to cut him with a knife! Daddy

was a strong man. He survived.
Forty-five when he died, correct.

No, the doctor did not tell him it was TB. Mommy hid it
from us, but I suspected. He lost so much weight. I took
care of him. I checked his temperature morning and
evening, but he did not want us spending time and effort
keeping him alive. Would not allow them to collapse his
lungs. He encouraged me to apply for medical school. It is
all right. I would take care of birds that fell from our *neem*
tree. Poor things, they were so frightened. It is all right. I
did not get in.

TECHNICOLOUR

I AM DISCOVERING speech under Mascarene skies. My father lives in America and plans to raise me there, so he asks my grandmother to teach me English instead of their mother tongue. This is why, when I later live with my mother, while we wait to rejoin him, she takes me to only American movies. *The Swiss Family Robinson* races ostriches, battles pirates. *Sleeping Beauty* sleeps under blue American skies. But I want to see an Indian movie, a film. What happens in an Indian film?

Swearing me to secrecy, my grandmother takes me. It's in her mother tongue. It's in black and white. In an early scene, Lord Krishna reclines on a window ledge and plays his flute. Villainous guards swing their swords at him, perhaps through him, in vain. In the final scene, warriors on horseback assemble in a courtyard while the evil king, mortally wounded, crawls to his death. The warriors cheer their new king and fireworks burst over the palace. White fireworks, in a black and white sky.

TEMPLE BAY

ON THE BEACH at Mahabalipuram, sand crabs play jute with the sea. *It's a game we played as children,* I say. *If the one who was It came too close, you could squat with a hand on your head and yell, "Jute!" and you couldn't be tagged.* So it is now while the sun sets: the world cannot touch us.

Last night, returning from the Shore Temple after photographing its towers, we prayed the long dark streaks taunting us meant no harm. Now we see it's true: dun crabs peering from holes run toward waves cresting pink, then back, swerving to evade water. Laugh: we laugh until one, the largest yet, heads right out to sea and vanishes. Others follow. We decide they know what they're doing.

In the morning this sea – in fact a bay, the Bay of Bengal – is green. Pale green where waves curl back onto themselves. Afternoon, it's blue. Now it's electric blue, electric green; olive drab where it churns the sand. Coppery. If we place our feet just so, the sand changes colour in halos like all the footprints of gods you photograph. Imagine: the weight of our passing leaves auras.

You: *Look at those clouds!* Massing above the sea, their centres white, a misty pink at the edge – translucent clouds veiling a blue streak. Now butterflies appear from the sun. They skim the dunes and also head out to sea. They'll come back. They're safe in places like this, where elements meet. Sun. Sea. Sand. Sky. At times like these. Twilight. Dawn.

At *Kanyakumari,* you say, *where this bay meets an ocean and a sea, on the evening of the full moon, you can watch sunset and moonrise together. Both at once?* I ask; then, *We'll go there, yes, one day.* For now, I can't imagine being anywhere but here.

Oh! you say. *Look.* From where we stand, the temple towers have overlapped. One triangle where before there were two. Fishermen claim the gods Vishnu and Shiva lived here. Durga as well. Three gods in one temple. But there's more: fishermen say that once there stood seven temples. The sea claimed the other six – intact, still, underwater. Fishermen know these things.

Tonight the moon will be almost full, more dazzling than we've seen it back home. That man in the moon will look less surprised, more knowing somehow. Tonight Venus will rise above her own reflection. But that's not all. She will glide ashore. If she places her feet in the auras of our passing, it will mean we are still in love.

Unaccompanied Cello Suites

You, by the window, read of art history from ancient Harappa's Lord of the Beasts to the Taj Mahal. Pause to watch the present pass: hedgeplants, sugar cane. Rest your eyes on type, the safety of numbered pages. And here we are jolting inland to the holiest hill in the South. Yes, getting there is half the fun, but India's too much in me to read. Or sightsee. I take refuge in your Walkman while speakers blare Bhangra pop, Tamil pop. *Han han aam aam yeah yeah.* Indians are not only stone deaf, they're tone deaf.

Slowing. Unscheduled. You, pulling me: *Look at this!* You see a man crouched like a monkey. Not just any monkey: Hanuman himself. Complete with golden mace, golden skin, monkey jaws blending oh so prosthetically into a red monkey face. *Can you not give money, ladies? Even a little, gents?* Bloody guide. Wouldn't answer questions about my family god. All aflutter now, all agog. *He is debasing himself, poor fellow, to raise necessary funds. To raise Hanuman temple for his village.*

You, coaxing: Let's give a bit. Meaning, if I can't spare rupees I can part with a smile. Rupees then. You try handing a five to the guide grasping spontaneous offers – mainly twos – but you're too late. He's out, he's back. Hanuman waves his thanks. And when a pale green note flutters from your window, he bows over clasped hands. You, ecstatic: He was perfect. You should've seen him! But I did, I insist, though not really: a flash of paint, a monkey face, a flick of ropey tail. I leave you with reflections of an India I can't face, even glassed in. You leave me to Yo-Yo Ma. The melody and broken chords of a sarabande.

⟶⚜⟵

We, on Commercial Street, spend our last night in my home town buying mirror work, *churidar* sets, Narayan's *The Emerald Route* – in cantonment, the British preserve where, after the Raj, my mother bought me clothes at Kiddie's Corner. We're spending rupees we can't take with us. Split up to splurge efficiently. You, alone, encounter an Indian Santa ringing his cowbell. An honest-to-god Santa Claus I miss while keeping an eye out for our hired car inching through crowds. Not Christmas shoppers; Commercial Street's always busy after dark. *Grotesque*, you say. *A gunny-sack belly, a rat's-nest beard, sweat streaking his greasepaint face, brown showing through made-up white skin.* You, appalled: *He was so grotesque. Too bad you missed him.*

Now that, yes, I wish I had seen. All the same, it's not true I don't see things. I simply don't share so much till later, when of course I share too much. Although once, on our verandah while you slept in that posh cabin at Mahabalipuram, you'll never believe what I saw. The Shore Temple grew distinct under a rising moon – hardly unusual, till the sea people started coming shore. They were dark. They left their boats to wade though shoals with lions, tigers, cheetahs. Surged back for elephants while those lumbering cats paced in the surf. Dark. They were dark even thirteen hundred years ago.

I came this close to waking you.

Acknowledgements

I wrote this book between 1983 and 1991 and kept revising it until 2015, during which time I also read widely in various genres and pursued my interest in photography. The following agencies provided me with generous writing support: the Department of Canadian Heritage, The Canada Council for the Arts, and the Saskatchewan Arts Board. I also held posts as a writer in residence that were supported by The Canada Council for the Arts, the Scottish Arts Council, the Department of English at the University of Alberta, and the Yukon Public Libraries. Finally, and early on, the Banff Centre for the Arts gave me a scholarship to the May Writing Studios, where I received advice and encouragement from the fiction writer and playwright Rachel Wyatt and the poets Don Coles and Anne Szumigalski.

Portions of this book have been previously published. Chapters, excerpts, and photographs have appeared in my poetry collection, *The Lightness Which Is Our World, Seen from Afar* (Frontenac House, 2006); in two anthologies, *Lodestone: Stories by Regina Writers* (Fifth House, 1993) and *Our Fathers: Poetry and Prose* (Rowan Books, 1995); in a textbook, *Insights: Immigrant Experiences* (Harcourt Brace Canada, 1995); and in the following magazines: *absinthe, Border Crossings, The Capilano Review, Dandelion, Event, Geist, Grain, Other Voices, Paragraph, Passages, The Photo Pipeline, Possibilitiis, Prairie Fire,* and *West Coast Line*. My thanks go to all of these editors, especially Rose Scollard of Frontenac House.

Finally, thanks go to my ex-wife, Shelley Sopher, for her patience and insights when I began this book and continued revising it during the many years of our marriage.

The passage from B.S. Johnson's *Introduction to Aren't You Rather Young To Be Writing Your Memoirs?* is reproduced with kind permission from MBA Literary Agents, Ltd. of London, U.K.

The passages from B.C. Deva's *Musical Instruments* (National Book Trust, India, 1977) are on pages 1-2.

Buddha's speech is on page 40 of *Buddhism* by Christmas Humphreys (Penguin Books Canada, 1978).

The line from *Family Ties That Bind* (International Self-Counsel Press, 1984) is on page 107.

ABOUT THE AUTHOR

Photograph by Don Hall

VEN BEGAMUDRÉ was born in South India and came to Canada when he was six. He has an honours degree in public administration and a master of fine arts in creative writing. He has held numerous residencies and was the 1996 Canada-Scotland Exchange Writer-in-Residence. His work has appeared in Canada, the United States, the Netherlands, and Scotland. He lives in Regina, Saskatchewan, and has lived in a number of countries including Bali. *Extended Families: A Memoir of India* is his ninth book.

ENVIRONMENTAL BENEFITS STATEMENT

By printing this book on FSC-certified recycled paper,
COTEAU BOOKS
ensured the following saving:

Fully grown trees	Litres of water	Kg of solid waste	Kg of greenhouse gases
0.77	2 803.81	34.37	314.77

These calculations are based on indications provided by the various paper manufacturers.

 Manufactured at Imprimerie Gauvin
www.gauvin.ca

Printed in July 2017
by Gauvin Press,
Gatineau Québec